REAL MEN DON'T APOLOGIZE!

REAL MEN DON'T APOLOGIZE!

JIM BELUSHI

NEW YORK

Library of Congress Cataloging-in-Publication Data has been applied for

ISBN: 1-4013-0182-7

Hyperion books are available for special promotions and premiums. For details contact Michael Rentas, Assistant Director, Inventory Operations, Hyperion, 77 West 66th Street, 11th floor, New York, New York 10023, or call 212-456-0133.

FIRST EDITION

10   9   8   7   6   5   4   3   2   1

A list of permissions, constituting a continuation of the copyright page, appears on pp. 271–272.

To my wife, Jenny . . .

CONTENTS

BOOK THREE
THE BOOK OF LOVE, ACCORDING TO JIM
167

ACKNOWLEDGMENTS

IF YOU WERE WONDERING WHO THE HELL THOUGHT JIM BELUSHI SHOULD WRITE A BOOK

I'll admit it. What initially attracted me to the idea of writing a book were two words: "Easy Money." Two years and twenty drafts later all I have to say is writing a book is a real bitch. It amazes me how quickly Bob Woodward made up all the bullshit about John for his book— Sorry, sorry, another time.

Anyway, this tome would never have been in your hands if it weren't for the dedication and support of a number of people. God knows, I would have packed it in if it weren't for them.

Bob Miller at Hyperion: He took the initial leap of faith and provided me with a great title. And he got someone to write me a big, fat check.

Leslie Wells at Hyperion: For her edits (and for not cutting out the filthy stuff). How great is it that this book was edited by a woman!

Every single member of the cast and crew of *According to Jim* deserves my recognition, but I have trouble remembering names so I just want to mention a special group of writers. Ron Hart, John Beck, David Feeney, Chris Nowak and Harry Hannigan are funny-ass guys. The humor in this book comes from their writing, their banter, their thoughts and their mistakes. Their dedication to *According to Jim,* and to me, really sparks a joy in my belly. And I know each one of them came up with a homophobic joke about sparks of joy in my belly. I wouldn't have even started without them.

Josh Young: He turned my insane and often drunken ramblings into something coherent, mixing the words with a great comic sensibility. When I would get stuck I'd say, "Ahhh, Josh, you've got to come up with something here and fix it for me." And the dude would. Could not have been done without him. I'd mow his lawn if he asked me. Well . . . I'd pay someone to mow his lawn.

My agent, Eddy Yablans, had to convince me five times that he wasn't going to let me get out of doing this book. He saw a book where I didn't see one. Now that I'm finally finished, I am grateful for his persistence in pushing me along. I'm always grateful for his resilience, his deep devotion to me and his superb friendship. And I know he will agree with me that my mentioning him in the acknowledgments is worth more emotionally than his ten percent of my cut.

Marc Gurvitz: He is a manager of the highest order. He manages with perception, insight and friendship and does it all with concern and thoughtfulness, even when I disagree with him. A man of true character. If he answered my calls, I'd tell him myself.

My assistant, Dena Reifschneider, who will piss in my coffee more than she does already if I don't mention her.

My cousin Gus has spent enough time listening to me to qualify as my therapist. I thank him for his devotion, his loyalty and his deep concern for my well-being. I also make no jokes about him as he has entirely too much dirt on me.

Stevie B: Ahhh, without Stevie B. there is no growth for me as a man. Every time he speaks I receive another pearl of wisdom. He is all present in this book because he belongs here, in the middle of the battle between men and women. Funny, insightful, strong. His stories sold the book in the first place. Which in no way means he'll ever see a dime from me.

The Coyote men's division: These were the first men to get me back on my feet and steer me in the right direction. They gave me the tools and the understandings that have guided me on this bumpy dirt road. They truly taught me what it's like to be supported by men.

My brother John. The first man I ever knew.

My son Robert. His mere existence is what motivated my intensity to grow as a man.

Jared and Jami: My two youngest children, who are rapidly generating material for my next book . . . *Marriage, Fatherhood, Divorce, Marriage, Fatherhood.*

REAL MEN DON'T APOLOGIZE!

BE ALL THAT DITKA
SAYS YOU CAN BE

Before you scoff and say to yourself, "What advice can Jim Belushi, beloved international superstar of stage and screen, give to me, Joe Everyman?" the answer is simple: hope.

I want to let you in on a little secret: I wasn't always the man you see today. There was a time in my life, believe it or not, when I was at rock-bottom. I was a loser. And it's because of those experiences that I'm able to relate to you guys out there looking for a little guidance, a little help. So, newsflash, kids: I am Joe Everyman. And to illustrate my point, I'm gonna tell you a story about a gourmet dinner I had with Mike Ditka.

Let me set the stage. The year was 1987, and I was working on a little film called *Red Heat*. You don't remember? Maybe this will refresh your memory: "Moscow's toughest detective. Chicago's craziest cop. There's only one thing worse than making them mad. Making them partners."

Ahhh, now you remember. Back then I was a major film star slumming with a little-known Austrian bodybuilder who needed a break.

Not a year earlier, my beloved Chicago Bears had danced the triumphant Super Bowl Shuffle, but they failed to repeat—losing to a New York Giants squad that we would later learn was all hopped up on coke. The loss saddened me greatly and the film's director, Walter Hill, visited me in my trailer to cheer me up.

Walter told me he'd just had a dream about a movie for me to make. In this movie I play myself. The film begins at my breakfast table. My wife is serving me six eggs over easy and three Polish sausages, but I cannot eat because I am too distraught over the apparent end of the Bears dynasty. Finally, she drops the frying pan and says, "Just do it. Just go join the Bears."

Realizing it is what I must do, I leave immediately for Bears training camp. Upon arriving, I explain to Coach Ditka that I want to contribute to the team. Because I am a noted linebacker from my high school years, he agrees to give me a shot. I spend several months training for opening day, and Ditka rewards me with a spot on the kickoff coverage team.

On opening day against the hated Packers, I race down the field during kickoff to cover the return man. As I'm zeroing in on the guy, a Packer blocks me out of the play. I tumble out of bounds, blowing out my knee. It is a career-ending injury, but I am happy because, for that brief moment, I played like a Monster of the Midway.

When Walter was finished speaking I said, "That's the greatest goddamned movie pitch I've ever heard. Get me five million plus ten percent of the gross and we can start shooting tomorrow." Walter left the trailer, and I was soon called to the set for my scene.

I should note, however, that as I was walking to the stage, I passed my costar's trailer and heard Walter's voice from inside: "Arnold, I had a dream. You're at your breakfast table, but you're depressed. Finally Maria says, 'Just do it. Just go run for governor.'"

My agent passed on Walter's brilliant idea and had me make *Homer and Eddie* instead. Remember that one? Me neither. But as fate would have it, a few years later I was invited to have dinner with Mike Ditka. As I watched him eat a steak thicker than my arm, I told him that someone had once pitched me an idea for a movie where he would be my costar.

As I recounted Walter's movie to Coach—it's a little thing Ditka and I have; I call him "Coach" and he calls me "Belutchi"—I was pretty sure he was more interested in his twice-baked potato than the story. But when I reached the part where I get blocked out of the play, Coach dropped his fork.

For a split second I thought he might need the Heimlich, but then he sprang from his seat (with surprising agility for a man who hasn't had cartilage in his knees since the sixties) and stuck his meaty index finger in my face. "No, Belutchi!" he bellowed. "You run down that field and you make that tackle. You force a fumble! You pick up the ball. You run into the end zone for a touchdown! You spike the ball! Because NO ONE REMEMBERS A LOSER! THEY ONLY REMEMBER A WINNER." That's why Coach Ditka has won a Super Bowl and Walter Hill hasn't.

No one remembers a loser. Write it down so you'll remember it. Oh, right. I wrote it down for you. But remember it, because truer words have never been spoken.

Believe me, I know. I've been a loser. I'll admit it; my career has had some peaks and valleys. The peaks being *About Last Night . . .* , *The Principal, Salvador, Taking Care of Business* (where the Cubs win the World Series!), and the ABC hit comedy *According to Jim* (Tuesdays at 8:00 p.m. Eastern, 7:00 Central and Mountain), with the valleys being . . . well, the nineties.

And, of course, the day my brother died.

At that moment not only did I lose a brother, I also became the head of the family, but I had no idea how to lead my family in the public spotlight. The media was capitalizing on my brother's death. My family and my life were falling apart, and I couldn't stop the downward spiral. I made one bad decision after another. One of those guys they quote for T-shirts once said, "Heroes aren't born, they're cornered." Oh, I was cornered. And I found out that I was no hero.

So I found myself in my late thirties with two failed marriages, a son I barely knew and a career circling the drain. My confidence was shot, my self-esteem was at an all-time low and just to fuck with me even more, God started thinning my hair.

Where am I today? I'm married to a woman I love and who (even more surprisingly) loves me too, and I have an amazing relationship with my older son. I have two more kids that I cherish and adore. I'm playing a part I love to play on *According to Jim,* and the public seems to really enjoy it. (Apparently critics don't have Nielsen boxes.) I get to tour the country with a ten-piece band, the Sacred Hearts, which blows the doors off any place they play. As for my hair . . . well, it's hanging in there.

Basically, I turned my life around. I pulled it kicking and screaming from the 99-cent used-VHS bin back to the actor-with-a-leading-role career. Only this time, I lived my life in a way that was true to the kind of man I wanted to be.

I didn't do it alone. I went to workshops to learn about being a man. I found a community of men to help me. And, most importantly, I discovered that only a man can teach another man what being a man is all about.

Fortunately for you, you've bought a book written by a man. So I'll give you the advice that I've collected from men like my friend Stevie B., Mike Ditka, my cousin Gus, David Deida, Robert Bly, probation officers, social workers, Rob Becker, Dr. Steven Benedict, shrinks, teamsters, headmasters, neighbors, the members of the Sacred Hearts Band (look for the CDs *36-22-36* and *Big Men, Big Music* on House of Blues Records) and A. Justin Sterling. It's a bit more in-depth than "No one remembers a loser," but that's your wake-up call.

This is a book about men, but not because I think men are better than women. Quite the opposite. Men are woefully outmatched by women. All men have to offer is our competitive instincts and whether or not we can lift something heavy. Women are nurturers, they literally carry life in them, they are community leaders, and they are intuitive, grounded, powerful, smart, verbal, complex and beautiful. It's tough to keep up with that. Both my previous marriages ended because I wasn't man enough for my wives.

I'm writing this book because we, as men, need to raise our game to meet the challenge the women of the world are giving us. The constant stream of challenges coming every single minute of every single day. Nothing but challenges. Hell, I can't even walk in the door before . . . all right. Let's hold that thought.

I want you to forget whatever you think you know about me as an actor and think of me as a man, like you. What I have to say might change your life. At the very least, it should help get you laid.

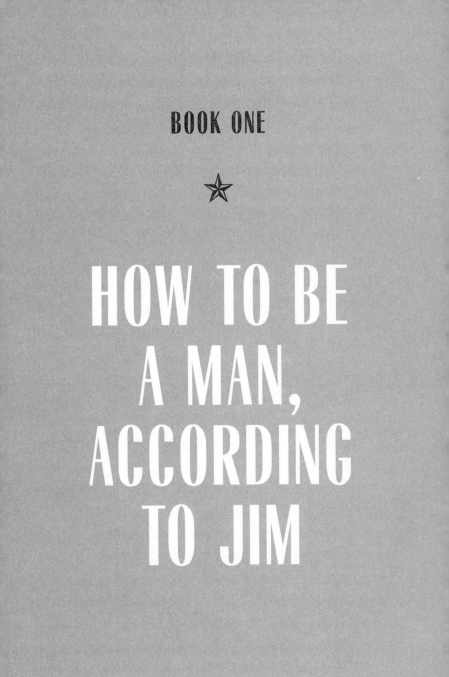

BOOK ONE

HOW TO BE A MAN, ACCORDING TO JIM

CHAPTER ONE

ARE YOU A MAN? TAKE THIS SIMPLE QUIZ

I'm a Man
I Spell "M"
"A" child
Nnnnn
Maaaaan

—"Mannish Boy," Muddy Waters and
Bo Diddley

The first thing I want everyone to know is, I am not a doctor. I am not a licensed therapist. I don't even play a doctor or licensed therapist on TV. I'm just a guy—and on TV I play a guy who is just a guy. Over the years, through making mistakes and paying attention, I have learned a few things about how to be a man, and how to conduct myself as a man in almost any situation. This is the information I want to share with you, but first, let's find out where you stand.

Take out a pen and keep score. Give yourself one point for every correct answer.

1. Check your groin for male genitalia. (Yes, now.) How many are attached to you?
   a. One.
   b. Zero.
   c. Other.

Give yourself one point for every penis. (If you score higher than one, skip ahead to the chapter titled "Are you a circus freak?") So far, so good. They get harder from here.

2. You are at work. Something goes wrong in your section. Do you:
   a. Blame the guy who doesn't speak English.
   b. Claim to have seen this coming and point out you warned somebody about this exact thing two weeks ago.
   c. Get a doctor to swear you suffer from a rare disorder that allows you to do all aspects of your job EXCEPT the one that keeps the thing that went wrong from happening.
   d. Take the hit, fix the problem, get back to work.

If you answered anything but d, you are exactly what is wrong with this country. Not only do you not get any points, but take away the one you got for having a penis.

3. You are having a fight with your wife/girlfriend. You have made your point, you've listened to her side. Now, you . . .

   a. Let her rehash it, telling you again why you piss her off/are wrong/don't friggin' get it.

   b. Leave the room.

   c. Bring up that thing she did New Year's Eve three years ago that you are still pissed about.

   d. Take her. Right there. Assuming it's not a fight over dinner in a restaurant you want to come back to.

If you said c and harbor a grudge from three New Year's Eves ago, then you are someone's ex-wife and should not be reading this. The answer is b (leave the room), or d (take her right there). If you don't know why, you are reading the right book.

4. Game seven of the (sport you like to watch) is on, but your girlfriend's cousin is getting married and your lady has already RSVPed for both of you. You:

   a. Tell her to have fun and bring you some cake.

   b. Bitch as you put your suit on, complain in the car on the way over, spend the whole event looking for a TV or at least the score.

   c. Go, be charming and gracious, stay as long as she wants, secure in the knowledge that she owes you. Big.

d. Chalk it up to relationship maintenance and try to have fun.

Surprise! There is no wrong answer here. Personally I would d because she has no ESPN to catch the wedding highlights, it doesn't compromise you as a man, and she'll be grateful for your sacrifice. Take away one point for not talking her cousin's fiancé out of getting married during the playoffs.

5. You're losing your hair. You deal with it by:
   a. Buying more ball caps.
   b. Fucking the babysitter.
   c. Calling the Hair Club for natural-looking implants.
   d. Deal with what? Who gives a shit about his hair?

Answer, d. If you are thrown by something as common, natural and meaningless as male-pattern baldness, you need more than this book—you need to hunt and kill your own food for a month.

6. You have been called by the government to lead a team of secret operatives to blow up a secret installation built into the side of a mountain where even our fancy high-tech bombs can't reach. You can have any three people, living or dead, on your team. You ask for:
   a. John Wayne, Ted Williams and Chuck Yeager.

b. A mountain climbing expert, a demolitions expert and someone who can speak the local language.

c. The three baddest motherfuckers you know.

d. Three guys you've known since you were kids.

Tricky, huh? You can learn mountain climbing, you can learn demolitions, and Ted Williams has his head frozen in a bucket somewhere, but priority one is guys you can trust, so the answer is d.

7. It's two in the morning and there is a loud party going on next door. You:

   a. Call the cops.

   b. Go over and ask them politely to keep it down.

   c. Go over in your bathrobe, announce that all the drunk girls can crash at your place and warn them that you have a tendency to sleepwalk naked.

   d. Try to get to sleep.

I think c is the only reasonable response. They're not going to keep it down if you ask nicely. It's a party!

8. Your friend is doing a reading at a poetry slam. You:

   a. Scream "You're doing a WHAT?!" Disavow him, and spend an hour looking in the mirror, wondering if you are secretly gay for being friends with that guy in the first place.

b. Make an excuse, stop taking his calls and slowly drift away from him. Wonder idly if he's gay. Sure he's married with three kids, but what about the poetry?

c. Sit him down over a beer and get the skinny. Is there a chick he's after there? Is this some kind of self-destructive thing? Give him constant (but good-natured) shit about it. Refer to him as Byron or Wordsworth (these are poets).

d. Go to the reading. Realize it's a competition. Make bets, talk trash, boo the bad poets. Paint your face like Byron or Wordsworth (again, they are poets). Bring beer. Burp a haiku (this is a short Japanese poem).

Another toughie. About now you are thinking, damn, I shouldn't have fallen asleep in the SAT preparation class. The correct answer is d, because if he has to "be him" and do poetry, then you have to be "be you" and fuck it all up for him.

9. You come out of a bar, and three guys are slapping around a smaller guy in the parking lot. You:
   a. Go back in the bar and tell the bouncer. It's his job.
   b. Keep walking. Small guys can be assholes. He probably deserved it.
   c. Join in. Either side, it doesn't matter. It's a fight! Hit someone!
   d. Stop the fight.

The Japanese samurai had a code that said never to take longer than seven seconds to make a decision. Most fights last about five seconds from the first punch to someone losing. Your response to this situation is pure instinct, and therefore it can't be wrong, but it can and does have consequences. You get one point if you chose one and stayed with it, and one more for going to a bar where fights break out.

10. Your friend and his wife are having a baby boy. She wants to name him "Tanner." You:
    a. Ask him if he needs to borrow a testicle until his wife lets him have his back.
    b. Congratulate him. Buy the boy books on choreography and fashion design.
    c. Nod sadly and suggest some nicknames for the kid: Spike, Nails and Bronco should be among them.
    d. Slap your friend and tell him he's a father. His job is to raise the boy to be a man. Tanner as a last name is fine. Tanner as a job is fine. Tanner as a first name sucks.

It's d. He may not see it, but your buddy's wife is making a power play. By naming the kid Tanner, she is taking him as her own and ensuring that he will never respect his father. You have to stop it now, or he is lost forever. She will say: "You're overreacting, it's a cute name. What's the big deal?" Men know instinctively that it's a big deal, and the kid will always resent them AND you if you don't do something. I'd recommend "Jim."

11. You go to the local theater, and four movies you've never heard of are playing. Based on the title, which will you like?
    a. *Camembert and Wig Powder*
    b. *Hotel Autumn*
    c. *A Sonnet for Lucinda*
    d. *O'Shea*

Even though I made them all up and you couldn't even look at the posters, the answer is d. It's a name, which means it's about a person. It's an Irish name, which means there's a really good chance he's a cop. Cop means guns, car chases and, if you're lucky, a supermodel who keeps changing clothes on camera.

12. You're with friends at a restaurant/bar and the bill comes. You:
    a. Quickly add up roughly what you had, add twenty percent (take ten percent, then double it).
    b. Take this opportunity to run to the bathroom.
    c. Throw too much money on the table.
    d. Get out a calculator, figure out what everyone owes to the penny. Gather everyone's card. Instruct the waitress how much to put on each card, so everyone gets charged for exactly what they owe.

This is a personal annoyance of mine. It's c, you tight-ass! You're with friends; they're not trying to screw you! Don't waste time figuring it out to the penny, and don't stick someone else with the check.

And now the scoring:

1–5: You are a Girly Man. No, wait, that still has the word "man" in it. That's too manly. You need to buy the book again because you'll need to read it twice. Not only are you not a man, you wouldn't even cheat on a quiz.

6–11: You are Mannish. A derogatory term describing a man who is not quite manly or a woman with gigantic hands. At this stage, you could be either of these things. So read this book. It will amuse you, it will make you think, and it will help you become more of a man. Plus it's paid for already.

12: You are a Cheater. There are men in the world who would score 12 on this quiz, but these men are not going to spend time taking a quiz written by a gruff-but-lovable TV actor. Adjust your score, 1 to 11.

All right. We've got a pretty good idea of who you are now, so let's start dispensing the wisdom.

CHAPTER TWO

WHAT IS A MAN?

Well every morning at the mine you could see him arrive.
He stood six-foot-six and weighed two-forty-five.
Kinda broad at the shoulder and narrow at the hips.
And everybody knew you didn't give no lip to Big John.
Big John.
Big John.
Big Bad John.

—"Big Bad John," Jimmy Dean

What is a man? A man has a set of franks and beans swinging between his legs, right? Well, guess what? So does your average male giraffe, and we all know giraffes are pussies. I mean, how can an animal that big only eat plants? I don't get it. So clearly genitalia aren't the only thing that defines what a man is.

So again, what is a man? Why do we have trouble defining ourselves now? I'll tell you why: Because as men, we do not know who we are anymore. We allow others to tell us how we should act, because we believe they are right when they tell us we are wrong. And we spend so much time listening to "how we shouldn't be" that we don't focus on "what we *should* be." Well, let's take a minute to talk about the kind of men we really shouldn't be—spineless, alone, unmotivated, unfulfilled, incomplete men. If only I could think of a good example of such a poor, unfortunate soul. Oh, I just thought of someone. The most pathetic excuse of a man I've ever met.

Me.

I was backstage at the Shubert Theatre in Chicago. It was 5:00 p.m., I was doing vocal warm-up for that night's performance of *Pirates of Penzance.* Yes, that's a musical and yes, I did have to wear tights, but wipe that smirk off your face and listen to my story.

The box office guy came backstage and told me they were saying "some weird things about John" on the radio, "like maybe . . . your brother's dead." I thought it was some *National Lampoon* type of joke like the Beatles when they did "Paul is dead." John and Danny were always pulling irreverent stunts. This one sounded just sick enough to be something they cooked up.

I called the station to rip into the deejay. I said, "This is Jim Belushi. What the fuck are you saying about my brother?" At first, he didn't believe I was really John's brother. When I convinced him he said, "I'm sorry, Jim, this just came across the AP wire." And he read it over the phone.

"John Belushi dead . . ." John always wanted to die young and leave a good-looking corpse. He got his wish.

I'd like to say that's the moment I grasped that I'd lost him, but I'm not sure I've ever grasped that. It still seems like he's around. How many times have I seen him in reruns of *SNL*, *Animal House* and *The Blues Brothers*? When my oldest son, Robert, cocks his eyebrows, I swear I see John. His presence and influence on me and on the industry was so immense. It just doesn't feel like he ever left.

It's not that I don't understand that he's dead. I mean, every day at least one person stops me to say they loved my brother. And let's be honest, have you ever read anything about me that didn't contain the sentence, "Jim Belushi, brother of the legendary John Belushi who died of a drug overdose at the Chateau Marmont . . ." Can't write an article about Jim Belushi unless you mention drug overdose *and* the Chateau Marmont. My family really ought to get a kickback for all the free advertising we've given that hotel.

So yeah, I get that he's dead. But I still don't feel like he's gone. A couple hours after that phone call I was onstage with a black armband; you know, the-show-must-go-on bullshit, I guess.

When I made it home, my family was suddenly asking me what *I* was going to do. All of the logistics for the funeral, the press and life had to be figured out. The immediate issue at hand was how we were going to get to the funeral, who was going to pay for it, who was coming, all that nightmare stuff you have to deal with when someone dies.

It's a Belushi family custom that whoever makes the most money in your family is the head of the family. It is also a Belushi family custom to make up Belushi family customs to back up your story when you're trying to make a point. I will let you decide which is which here. The bottom line is, I was the only one in my family who seemed to understand that I wasn't equipped to handle the job of being a leader.

The funeral was a mob scene. Everywhere I turned there were reporters, flashbulbs, video cameras, mobs of people, helicopters. I tried to be the rock for my family and the best thing I could figure out to do was to bring a pocketful of Valium. My sister started sobbing—slip her a Valium. My aunt is in hysterics—slip her one. My mom can make a scene at a quiet family dinner, and I was worried about what she would do in front of the tabloid vultures. I slipped her a Valium.

People magazine ran a picture of the funeral which showed my mother on the sidewalk outside of the church entrance, dressed in black, crunched over and clutching the crucifix from John's coffin. My first wife and I are each holding one of her arms. It's a classic portrayal of a mother in grief.

The thing is, she wasn't grieving. She was just pissed off, and . . . well, let's just say it. She was high. As soon as we left the church, she lost her balance and stumbled. My wife and I kept her on her feet. She turned to me and snapped into my ear, "What the hell did you just give me? I can barely walk." Right then, the photographer snapped the picture. My mom would later accuse me of cheating her out of her grief. Nobody in my family was ever worried about my

21

grief, but I was in charge and it was my first bad decision.

A few days later there was a memorial service at St. John the Divine in Manhattan. Afterward, John's manager, Bernie Brillstein, grabbed my brother Billie and me in the hallway of our hotel. The autopsy was over. The verdict was in: John died from an overdose.

After twenty years, it probably seems as if we should have known it was drugs as soon as we learned he had died. I'm telling you, it was a complete surprise to me. I mean John was overworked, he ate poorly, he was overweight, heart attacks run in my family. When Bernie told us it was drugs, it felt like John had died all over again.

Billie and I did exactly the same thing. We backed up until we hit the wall, then we slid down until we were both sobbing on the floor of the hotel. My ass hit the floor and it stopped, but in a real sense I kept sliding for years after that bombshell.

The decade that followed needs its own book to truly do it justice: the pain my family went through as our family hero became a notorious, mythological figure; the two marriages I tried and failed at because I couldn't stand up for myself; the son I didn't think I could be a role model for. When Bob Woodward's series of articles and his book *Wired* came out filled with gossip and bullshit instead of the exploration of John as a man and a talent my family had been promised, it felt as if John died all over again. They say a cat has nine lives; it was as if John had nine deaths. For years I was a complete mess.

As an actor, being the brother of John Belushi was both a blessing and a curse. The relationship opened doors that other actors couldn't get near. Although, once that door was opened, I had to be able to not just walk through that door, but to leap through it. At every meeting and in every job I had after that, the pressure to live up to my last name was enormous. And critics never forgave me for not being as good as John. But who was? He was a huge star. He was a legend. Shit, I was the guy's biggest fan. Every one of us comic actors were. And, really, I was more of a fan than a brother.

A lot of people don't realize this, but we weren't that close growing up. Think about it—when he was in eighth grade, I was in third grade. You know any eighth-graders that want to hang out with their eight-year-old brothers? And he was long gone by the time I got to high school. Sure, he was family, but in a way I only knew him the way the rest of the country did. We didn't start becoming close until right before he died.

But since I could never escape his legacy, I had to create a new standard, and it had to be damn good. If I told a joke, it had to be three times as funny as anyone else telling the same joke. Today I could go on *Inside the Actors Studio* and talk about how that challenge helped me create a backbone for myself (that is, if *Inside the Actors Studio* ever returned my freaking calls!). But for years John's legacy felt like a cross I had to bear, and I lashed out in a lot of different arenas in my life.

I got angry; I screamed; if the fries weren't hot enough, I yelled at the fry girl; if I got cut off on the freeway, I'd follow the jackass home; I drank too much; and once, when I was on *SNL*, I threw a fire extinguisher at the show's producer, Dick Ebersol. I even pulled a knife on Larry David backstage at *SNL*. It was a joke, but I don't think he "got it." Worst of all, I cut off my family and just let everyone in my life drift away from me.

Some famous guy once said, "You only get good judgment from experience. And you only gain experience from bad judgment." If that's true, then I'm the most experienced guy on earth. Years into my life, I kept making the same mistakes over and over again. Like many guys, I went through life undefined. The proverbial house built upon sand. Now, bonus points for anyone out there who can tell me what proverbial means. Yeah, I don't know either. I just hear guys like Dennis Miller say it a lot.

When I told my good friend Stevie B. I was getting divorced for the second time, he sat me down. I listened because Stevie B. has been my friend for years, and I have come to know him as "the ultimate man." He owns a chain of rib joints. How cool is that? Rich, and buys meat by the ton. He once challenged Muhammad Ali to a fight. The champ was a hundred feet away and I'm not sure he heard Stevie B., but trust me, Stevie B. was ready to throw down. Still not convinced? How about this: Stevie B. once managed to pull off a three-way in the lavatory of a 747 flying from Chicago to Miami. That's like three hours of air time. That's a man.

Am I using the word "man" a lot? That's because Stevie B. kept ranting, "When the hell are you going to grow up and become a man?" I wasn't happy, but I couldn't see what Stevie B. could see. And that was that—I was at rock-bottom.

He took me out, got me hammered, and told me he was going to make me a man. To do that, he told me I had to define what kind of man I wanted to be. I told him I didn't have to figure it out; I already knew what I wanted to be. He told me there was a big difference between knowing what you want to be and defining it.

Think of it this way. If you asked a kid what he wanted to be when he grew up and he answered "a rich athlete," your next question would be, "Oh, yeah? What sport?" If the kid answered, "I don't know, whichever one wants me," you'd tell the little creep he needs to be more prepared if he wants to reach his goal. Does he think Iron Mike Ditka just decided one day he was gonna be the toughest tight end ever to play the game, and then just went out and did it without working at it first? Okay, bad example; Ditka probably did just that. But let's face it, none of us are Ditka.

The kid has a goal in mind, but he has yet to develop his definition of himself. This kid needs to identify a few things that define his goal. Like what sport he's good at. Say he picks football. Then he needs to decide what position he would like to play, what position he's suited for, what position will get him laid the most. If he doesn't define what it is he wants to be, someone else will do it for him and make him into what they want him to be. And you know what that means . . . Special Teams. And the guys on Special Teams never get laid.

We as men need to take back our sense of self, define who we are and stand by it, instead of listening to what other people want us to be and then trying to stuff ourselves into that mold. That's like letting someone talk you into putting on that Speedo you wore on the high school swim team. (Wait, were you really on the swim team? Oh, boy . . .)

Stevie B.'s first assignment for me was to make a list of my *agreements with myself* that I need to hold sacred. A. Justin Sterling calls these **terms**. Every man must sit down and ask himself, "What are the six things I would kill for if someone tried to take them away from me?" And I don't mean the beers in your six-pack. These are your terms. Your terms are the sum total of who you are as a man. They are your defining characteristics. You must defend these terms with your last dying breath, or your life will come crumbling down around you.

You think I'm being overly dramatic? Hey, I'm an actor. That's what I do. But I could not be more serious about this. Once you figure out what is important to you, you have to stand by it.

Most men have not defined who they are, and have not come up with their terms. This is especially unattractive to women. They don't want a shapeless nothing. That's like that baggy pair of pants they wear the day after they binge on ice cream. They hate those pants because it means they've been weak. They want a man who's like the pair they wear that makes their ass look good. They love those pants because they can go out in the world and people will say "nice pants." If you don't know who you are, how can you make her ass look good?

Here is the list of terms I came up with: Work. Integrity. Respect. Family. Loyalty. Self-honesty. When I told Stevie B. I had made my list, he was shocked that I had finally started to take control of my life. He even said he was proud of me. Moments later, he threatened to crush my windpipe if I told anyone he said it. I love that guy.

How did I come up with my terms? I thought about all the things that pissed me off over the years and all the times I allowed myself to be compromised and boiled them down into categories I knew I wanted to change about myself, and categories I saw in other people's lives that I did not want for mine. Most importantly, I thought about a movie being made of my life and how I would want the main character to be written. Long story short, I'd rather be Indiana Jones than Woody Allen.

Work. Yes, I consider acting work. Nothing ever takes precedence over my work because it's part of who I am. To entertain is my higher purpose. Nobody gets in the way of my work. Nobody, friends, family, nobody. I've gotten rid of girlfriends and wives over this. Here's a great example: I smoked cigarettes and cigars for twenty-five years. People always told me to quit; I even tried a couple times, but I always went back. Then a few years ago I realized the smoking was affecting my voice. That's a bad thing for an actor, but a career killer for a singer. So I gave it up. And just to underscore how important this was to me: I had my own line of cigars (by the way, if you need a gross of cigars real cheap I've still got some inventory left over).

Every man needs a higher purpose. Your higher purpose may not be what you do for a living. But if it's not, you should look for another job.

Integrity. I didn't put this on my list because I want to be the most honest man on the planet. Those of you who know me are aware that I am, by no means, as honest as Abe Lincoln. (Typically, I only try to be as honest as Nixon. I mean, he was honest like 90 percent of the time.)

If I'm going to do something slightly off-center, I'm going to do it for myself. Not for someone else. I used to cover for people all the time and then get caught in their lies, trying to make them look good while making myself look like an ass in the process.

Once the wife of a buddy of mine called me and asked if her husband was having an affair. I, of course, answered no, and feigned shock and righteous indignation that this woman could even suspect an upstanding man like my buddy of cheating. My buddy, of course, was having the affair. Worse, he was making no effort to keep it a secret. The cover story he gave to his wife was that he was going to the gym. The hole in his plan was that he gained thirty pounds. The chick he was cheating with was one hell of a cook. So, of course, he eventually got caught. But as luck would have it, he and his wife worked it out and fell deeply in love again. Guess who was the asshole? Not my buddy for cheating. Nope, it was me for lying. His wife deemed me a "bad influence." That's what you get for covering for someone else. Shit, even the woman he was cheating with was pissed at me. You'd think she'd be a little more appreciative, considering that I had introduced the two of them.

What really bothers me is being asked to lie about stupid stuff. I answered a past girlfriend's phone once. It was her dentist. He was calling to ask why she was late for her checkup. She freaked. She had forgotten the appointment. And this girl hated confrontations—with everyone except me. Not wanting to look like a scatterbrain, she told me to tell him she was not feeling well because her grandmother had just died. Come to think of it, she wasn't well, but this was no different from any other day in her life.

Now, why lie in this situation?! It's the goddamned dentist, not a grand jury. (Well, I might lie to a grand jury, depending on what Stevie B. was accused of.) I decided not to lie for her. I told the dentist she was just lazy and overslept. Lost the girl, but kept my integrity and was glad about it. One day it's the dentist, next day it's hiding a body. No thanks.

Respect. I will never associate myself with anyone who will make me look like a fool in public. That doesn't mean I won't make myself look like a fool. I mean, half my career is dancing around with my shirt off, for Christ's sake. But there's a difference between someone who is goofing around with you and someone who is making themselves look good at your expense.

Sometimes you have to earn respect the old-fashioned way—with your fist. I will never forget the day I knew I had earned my brother John's respect. John was out partying, and we were getting concerned because he had a meeting the next morning. So I was sent to find him and bring him home. After checking his normal haunts, which was a pretty cool circuit to visit, I finally found John at an apartment party. I told him it was time for him to go home, and coaxed him out of the building. Given how much fun he was having at the party, he was surprisingly cooperative. Then all of a sudden he stopped.

"Wait a minute, wait a minute, Jimmy," he said. "Let's talk for a minute. We're brothers. Come on. We're gonna talk like people talk."

I knew that this was the start of the "John Con." A little smile was forming on his lips and he was giving the key words a little lift of the eyebrow. He didn't want to talk to me. He saw the tunnel on his night closing quickly, and he wanted to keep it going. He started working me. He was telling me what a great time *we* could be having at the party. Maybe there was an even better party.

"John, it ain't happening," I said, cutting him off. "We're going home. I'm bigger than you now and we're goin' in."

"Wait a minute, wait a minute. I'll tell you what," he said, beginning his last-ditch effort. "We'll fight. We'll have a fistfight. If you win, I'll go home with you. And if I win, you come out with me. Deal?"

Are you fucking kidding me? You're damn right we had a deal! I had been waiting for this moment ever since he punched me when I was in the eighth grade because I stole from his penny collection. As I sat there with a bag of Green Giant over my eye, I swore one day I would kick his ass. That day had arrived!

"Sure, John. Deal."

So we started circling up, with our fists moving around in front of our faces.

"This feels like *East of Eden*," he said. I had to see the movie again before I knew what the hell he was talking about.

Finally I took my shot and popped him right in the mouth. Rather than fight back, he dabbed his bloody lip and then screamed, "Are you crazy?! I'm an actor, you don't punch an actor in the face! That's it. You win."

"Oh, come on, John, the fight's just getting started," I said.

"No, that's it. Jimmy's the tough guy. Tough guy Jimmy wins! I'm just little John with a bloody lip. You're the winner! I'm the loooooser."

"But this is my shot to beat the shit out of you," I protested.

"Nope, you win. You beat me up. Let's go."

Shit! He snuck out of a beating. I was shocked. I won?

Just before we reached the entrance to my apartment, he

once again started working me to stay out a little longer. No parties, he promised, just two brothers hanging out. I agreed and we went for a ride in my Jeep. (Hey, it was a cool car in 1980. Enjoy your Mini Cooper, jerk.)

As I drove up Clark Street, he picked up a Polaroid camera that was on the floor of my car. At a stoplight, John ripped open the door as if he were about to jump, leaned way out of the car, and snapped a picture of a guy waiting for the bus in front of Steak and Egger. Then he shut the door, looked at me, and said, "That was cool."

That night, we went up and down Lake Shore Drive, and all through Lincoln Park, stopping at the totem pole on Montrose so he could snap some Polaroids with me in front of the totem pole. We dropped in on Blues, a bar on Halsted. We didn't drink or party. We just hung out, and it was the single best time I ever had with my older brother. And why? Because I knew he respected me.

Family. Remember how I said I wasn't any good at being the head of the family? Well, once I got my shit together, I looked around and realized my family situation couldn't get much worse. Why not be the guy in charge? My family was in chaos and I didn't like it. Someone had to step up.

Let's face it. Family is the one thing that you do not get to choose in life. Bad news for the Menendez brothers, good news for Tito, Jermaine and LaToya. But when it all comes down to it, sometimes your blood is all you have.

The bottom line is that your family is your connection

to this Earth. And sometimes you don't realize that until after it has been taken away from you.

Loyalty. There are, however, people whom you do get to choose. Your friends. Your business associates. Your girlfriends/wives. Your sports teams. Even when they have let you down every year since 1908. Even when Leon Durham can't open his glove because Gatorade was spilled on it in 1984, and they blow a two-game lead in a five-game series to the Padres. Even when some dumbass with headphones reaches over the wall and kills your chance of going to the World Series.

Now, loyalty can be a tough one between guys when there are chicks around. Be careful, you should never be chasing the same girl as your buddy. If you are competing with a friend over a woman, the stakes in your one-on-one basketball games are not high enough. At the first sign of tension, the girl has to go.

Self-honesty. I know what you're saying. "What in the blue hell does 'self-honesty' mean?" Admitting you have a small Johnson? No. It's much more serious. At least in my life, this is the most important term of them all. Be honest with yourself about who you are. And then never, *ever* apologize to anyone for being that man.

Real men don't apologize for being who they are.

People say they are sorry far too often for things they are not truly sorry about. "Sorry I'm late. I got caught in traffic." You're not sorry you're late! You're pissed off you're late! It's okay to be pissed off. Don't apologize for that. "I'm sorry I offended you when I said you were being a nag." No, you're not! You're damn glad you finally had the balls to tell someone to get off your damn back! "I'm sorry I farted." No, you aren't. You only wish it had lasted longer and more people got to smell it. Stuffy people.

"Sorry" is a lie. Unless, of course, you did something malicious that you felt badly about later. But otherwise it's such a manipulative word. You are trying to ingratiate yourself to others by saying "sorry," instead of being proud of who you are. But never say you're sorry for being who you are. Be proud of who you are, damn it! And if someone can't deal with the person you are, it's time to find someone else to hang out with. As long as you are honest with yourself and those around you, *they* have no right to make *you* apologize for being yourself.

"Never say anything about anybody that you wouldn't say to their face." That's more than just a sentence with a host of grammatical agreement problems. That's the simple rule I follow to make sure I'm maintaining self-honesty, integrity and loyalty.

After I told Stevie B. my terms, I asked him what was on his list. He said it was similar to mine, but that he had "blondes" and "cable" on there, too.

Developing these terms is the first step in defining who you are. The next step is knowing how to present this newly defined man to the world.

Read any expert on male identity, and they all say the same thing: A true man has different faces to use for different occasions. Your true definition is a combination of these sides of your personality. I like to compare it to a television set.

Remember those projection TVs from the eighties that some douchebag completely overcharged me for? Maybe you remember them from the sports bar. They projected the television image from three color tubes: red, blue and yellow (red, blue and ivory if you bought from my guy). These three colors would combine to form the complete image.

This televised image is like your maleness. It's something you project, and it's comprised of three different personalities. In different situations these personalities will blend differently. With the television, sometimes more red is needed for the picture, so that tube has to project more. You'll use your personalities in the same way. 'Course, usually it was a really shitty picture and you needed about 1,800 square feet in one room just to fit the sonofabitch. It's just a bad metaphor. I don't know why I'm using metaphors anyway, but at the very least I think I can now write off that TV set as "research."

Every real man I've ever talked to or read on the subject of being a man says the same thing. A true man has three essential elements of his personality: humor, compassion and strength. In my mind, A. Justin said it best: Every man has to have a little bit of Curly, Gandhi and Clint Eastwood in him.

Curly, a man's sense of humor. Ah, the Stooges. Men love 'em. Women don't get 'em. Wanna know why? 'Cause the Stooges embody what every man would love to be doing in a social situation where he doesn't want to be in the first place. Who wouldn't love to dump paint on his buddy's head or knock the ladder out from under him while he's chasing an escaped spider monkey? What guy wouldn't want to use a lobster claw to pinch a lady's ass or blow the cream out of a pastry into some rich guy's face?

Men need to have fun or we're bored—and boring. And, as I will discuss later, you can make a woman feel many different types of emotions—happy, sad, angry, embarrassed—but under no circumstances should you ever bore her.

Gandhi, a man's sense of compassion. This one is pretty simple. No one wants to be around a prick who doesn't give a damn about anything or anybody.

And when you care, get passionate! Look at Gandhi. There was a man who really cared about what he believed in. A hunger strike? Damn. Maybe it's just me, but I go crazy every day at about 3:30, just 'cause I can't see any way that I'll make it to dinner. Granted, Gandhi had it a bit easier because his people don't eat cows, so he didn't really know how great a burger would taste after his twenty-fifth day of hunger. But you get the idea.

Clint Eastwood, a man's sense of strength. How many times have we seen Clint ride alone into town with more guns trained on him than Jenna Jameson has sex partners? You know why? Because a Clint Eastwood character stands up for what he believes in and doesn't give a damn if anyone else stands with him or not. It's incomprehensible that he would not fight for what he believes in.

Why does this matter to you? I mean, you're not a cowboy. You're not a Marine. Please . . . Anyone who has been in an argument with his wife or girlfriend knows the odds are stacked so far against him, he might as well be the Cubs at the beginning of every season. Lots of hope, little chance. But do we cancel the season? Hell, no! We won in 1908 and if we keep on fighting, some day we might even win one again!

Clint always fights the good fight, and so should every man. It earns you respect from those around you. Also, chicks dig it.

Almost every guy has two of these three guys in his repertoire, but the third one is always missing. I was a master at the Gandhi. I could be a sympathetic basket case faster than most chicks. I had a very strong Curly as well because, as you know from watching my show every week, I'm hilarious. But Clint was never my strong suit. Despite what you saw on screen during *The Principal,* I am not naturally a badass.

When I would get in conflict with a woman I'd go all Gandhi. I'd become compassionate, understanding, start "listening to her feelings." When that didn't work, I'd pull the Curly and try to defuse the situation by joking about it. But sometimes those two wouldn't be enough. There are times when a woman really needs you to be a man with a backbone. They need you to be able to say no and hold your own positions. But I couldn't pull Clint out of my back pocket and stand up to them. I had to work long and hard to be the prick I am today.

Before we can get anything else right in our lives, we must first master these three personalities and learn when to use them. But if I sent you out into the world with just that, it'd be like going to play the Packers wearing only a jockstrap: a good start, yes, but not nearly enough in the big picture. I've laid out the framework of the man you can become, but that by no means makes you a man. Actually, becoming that man is going to involve some work. And that work starts in boot camp.

CHAPTER THREE

BOOT CAMP FOR MEN TRYING TO BECOME REAL MEN

She won't do this
She won't do that
She won't do nothing
'Til she knows where I'm at
Hey, hey look at what you did
You can call it what you want
But I call it messin' with the kid

—"Messin' with the Kid," Junior Wells

You're probably wondering why I call it boot camp. Well, it's the same reason the military calls it boot camp. Because you need a boot in your ass. [Simone, please Google boot camp and make sure that's the reason it's called boot camp—JB.]

Think of it this way. If you were drafted to go to World War II, they didn't just take you off the bus and drop you directly on the beach at Normandy. No, they sent you off down to Camp Dimbledebum [Simone, please insert name of famous basic training camp here—JB] to learn about being a soldier: how to march, follow orders, shoot a gun and all that military stuff from *Stripes*.

Before I forget, I'd like to take a moment to thank Simone. She's my researcher. My five-foot-nine, twenty-three-year-old dancer-turned-researcher. She came with Stevie B.'s highest recommendation (specifically, "you owe me, fucker, so just do it!"). I asked her to look up some of those WW II facts. Provided she did a good job, "thanks Simone." If she didn't, that means I stared a little too long at her ass the other day and pissed her off.

Actually, a better example of boot camp is *Full Metal Jacket*. In the first scene, the drill sergeant tells the recruits they "are nothing but unorganized grabastic pieces of amphibian shit." I'm stumped at coming up with a better way to describe you, my faithful reader. Perhaps you don't like being described as amphibian shit. Perhaps you are saying, "Hey, I'm bad off, but not as bad as you were, Belushi. You made three sequels to *K-9*, for christsakes."

Two things. Number one, a couple of those sequels were pretty damn good. You should rent them. Number two, don't think that because you aren't as famous as me that you can't bottom out like me. You may not have had a brother die on the pages of *People* magazine, but if you're reading this book, then there is at least a small part of you that somewhere identifies with what I'm talking about and that means you've been in a similar predicament. You've lost a job, a woman, a limb, or maybe it was a beloved family member. It's called hitting rock-bottom, because you're as low as you can go until all you can do is look up.

Just in case you're having a problem wrapping your head around the concept of rock-bottom, I'm going to give you an example. This time it's not my story. It's the story of an everyday guy who never made the cover of the *National Enquirer*.

I told you how Stevie B. made me sit down and define my terms and work on my presentation skills. This was just the first step in a long process. With his help and the guidance of several relationship gurus, I was able to move forward in the process of reestablishing myself. Part of that process, as you'll see in a little bit, was establishing a community of men to support me. Some of these guys, like Stevie B., really helped me. Some of the guys were a help to me because I could help them. But there was no one who needed more help than my friend Paul.

When I met Paul, he and his girlfriend Kate were trapped in a cycle of breaking up and reuniting. She'd dump him and he'd come crawling back to her, promising to live up to her impossible expectations of him.

Then she dumped him and told him this time it was for real. Something dawned on Paul—no more annoying laugh, no more endless late-night interrogations, just him. Alone. Panic set in. Kate was the only woman who ever loved him. What if no one else ever did? And she and he weren't all bad, right? They had their good times. Her laugh wasn't *that* annoying. And come on, who really needs to get a blow job on Mr. Toad's Wild Ride? Holy shit. He was alone and would always be alone. Paul was scared. He had to do something.

Now before I go on, I know what you're saying. "Paul is a giant pussy." "I certainly have never felt that way." Bullshit. We've all been there. We've all had that dead pit in our stomachs. And no, that's not beer swirling around down there, remnants of the five or six kegs you killed trying to forget her. It's her. And it's fear. What separates the Stevie B.s and Pauls of the world is what they do with this fear.

And what did Paul do? Well, it's a scene too filmic to write in prose form, so I'm going to write the following in script format—as if it were a movie.

FADE IN:

INT. KATE'S FRONT PORCH—NIGHT

PAUL WALKS UP TO THE FRONT DOOR AND KNOCKS. AFTER A BEAT, *KATE* OPENS THE DOOR.

KATE: Paul . . . ?
PAUL: Hello, Puddin'.
KATE: You know I hate it when you call me that.
PAUL: Sorry, babe.
KATE: That, too.
PAUL: Oh, right.
KATE: It's late. What are you doing here?
PAUL: I came here to give you something.

PAUL TAKES A BOX OUT OF HIS POCKET AND HANDS IT TO HER. *KATE* OPENS IT.

KATE: What's this?
PAUL: It's a ring. I want you to marry me.
KATE: Oh, my God. You're serious.
PAUL: See, I've been doing some thinking. And I realized something. I love you. I always have. Sure, we had our problems. But I think the real test of a couple is to see if we can work out those problems together. I want to be that couple. I want to be together. What do you say?

ROMANTIC, ORCHESTRAL MUSIC SWELLS AS *KATE* TAKES A SECOND TO THINK. *PAUL* WATCHES ON, A NERVOUS WRECK, BUT HE KNOWS HE'LL HAVE HIS ANSWER.

KATE: No fucking way.

KATE THROWS THE RING TO THE GROUND AND *SLAMS THE DOOR SHUT,* LEAVING *PAUL* ALONE AND DEJECTED. *HE* PICKS UP THE RING AND *EXITS OFF THE PORCH.* AS A LIGHT RAIN BEGINS TO FALL, WE:

FADE OUT.

Eat your heart out, Tarantino. Sure, putting the rain in there at the end was a little much, but originally I had her kicking him in the balls and keeping the ring.

Anyway, back to Paul. He's staring loneliness square in the face and what does he do? He proposes. He'd rather spend the rest of his life with a bitch than with himself. And look how badly it turned out for him. And do you want to know why? (This is why I wrote the scene like a script—boy, am I smart.) Because life ain't the movies! Romantic scenes like that only work on the big screen. They don't work in real life. In real life, you make an ass out of yourself and the girl slams the door in your face.

Paul's solution to his fear wasn't a solution at all. It was a temporary fix for a permanent problem—like putting cologne on a dirty wino instead of giving him a bath. Well, that doesn't make sense because I would never even give a wino a bath. I'd probably buy him a beer and send him on his dirty way . . . I'm losing my train of thought.

Like I said, we've all been this way—all of us except Stevie B. No way would Stevie B. ever propose to a woman just because he's feeling alone. Stevie B. never feels alone. That's because Stevie B. is the exception to the rule (by the way, I get a hundred bucks for every time I mention him in this book, so deal with it! Stevie B. Stevie B. Stevie B. Ha!). So what would Stevie B. do? If he ran into one of his exes, he would try to succeed in seducing her. It's called the "Getting the Upper-hand Lay."

Unless, of course, he ran into his ex from twenty-three

years ago. And the ex was with her daughter. Her twenty-three-year-old dancer-turned-researcher daughter. In that case, he wouldn't seduce the ex. Instead, he'd get his schmuck friend to overpay the twenty-three-year-old dancer-turned-researcher for a job she's not qualified for so that the "friend" could try to extract her DNA from a coffee cup or something for a paternity test. Why would he do this? Because he's oblivious to the fact that the twenty-three-year-old dancer-turned-researcher is hot as shit and the "friend" has a wife who is not blind. But he sure as hell wouldn't propose.

One by one, I want to beat these ideas into your head. Right now, you're at rock-bottom . . . just like Paul. Or like I was. So to help you climb up, dear reader, let me present *Belushi's First Rule to Climb Up from Rock Bottom:*

1. THINK OF YOURSELF FIRST.

Men can be self-centered. We usually think of ourselves first. But society has conditioned us to believe that we should think of ourselves last. I mean, look at what they've got us doing. All we do all day long is provide for other people. That's why we work. Working is providing for our wives, girlfriends, children, et al. (Okay, I got "et al" from my editor, who—gadzooks—is a woman. I originally had "ibid," but was quickly laughed out of her literary office.)

My point is, just because we've been programmed to be this way doesn't mean we have to be. In our daily lives—and, dare I say, in our love lives—we can be selfish. And that selfishness can help us become better men. We've earned this. We just have to learn, or relearn, how to do it. Of course, this is all just a fancy way of saying, "Never give up the remote."

Now for *Belushi's Second Rule to Climb Up from Rock Bottom:*

2. SURROUND YOURSELF WITH YOUR BUDDIES.

What if one day you look in the mirror, freshly dumped, and realize you have no idea who you are, outside your old relationship. Where does a man turn to learn who he is? What he wants? How to be a man? I'll tell you: to other men.

We're the answer. We're the ones who are going to set you straight. Women aren't going to do it. Movies and television sure as hell aren't going to do the job. (Except, naturally, a little program called *According to Jim.*) If you want to learn how to be a man, you should hang out with men. Sounds obvious, doesn't it? It's so obvious that you'd think more men would do it. But no, they don't. For christsakes, it took me forty years to learn this.

So what men do you turn to for this help, for this basic training? Your friends, of course. Your pals, chums, fellas, comrades, allies, joes, cohorts, dudes, boys, cronies, drinkin' buddies, wingmen, whatever you want to call 'em. They're your guys. They're the ones who are going to help you get back to thinking for yourself. Even all those guys you lost touch with over the years for whatever reason (her) and swore you'd never call them again because of a fight you had over something stupid (her). Call them up. You need those guys now. You need to form your own men's team.

A group of men must have rules. Through trial and error, my old buddies and I have come up with some critical rules for who's allowed in a men's group:

—He must love sports. Preferably, Chicago sports.

—He has to be able to take a punch in the gut. Because when you watch Chicago sports, you get agitated. Some guys eat when they're agitated. Me, I like to hit things. Mostly I go for couch cushions or drywall. But when it's the playoffs and our shortstop boots a simple groundball, I'm going to need to strike another man. If you're really my friend, you'll understand because, of course, I'm not going to apologize.

—He must love cheese. Think about it. Cheese is a critical food to a guy because it tops all foods eaten while attending sports or watching sports on TV. Pizza. Cheeseburgers. Nachos. Sushi. All right, most people don't eat cheese on sushi, but they should, because the stuff tastes like raw fish.

—He needs the ability to Shut the Fuck Up. There is nothing worse than hanging out with someone who thinks being quiet is anti-social. I can watch four hours of football with a close friend and only need to say: "Turn it up," "Pass the nachos," and "Christ, was that you? Open a window or something."

—He needs one physical liability. You must be slightly overweight, balding, have a lisp, a scar, or something that I know I can poke fun at if I need to shut you up because you're poking fun at something that really gets under my skin.

—He owns up to his own farts. I don't like smelling ass, but if I smell it, I'd better know whose hairy ass dealt it. If I let one loose in an elevator, I simply raise my hand and announce proudly: "Right here! That was me!" Being a man means taking pride in ALL your creations.

—He must be vulnerable. This might be the most important quality you're looking for. If these guys are going to help you, you're going to have to be vulnerable with them. And the only way you can trust them is if they are vulnerable with you in return.

That's our list. You can use it if you want. For twenty bucks. Make checks payable to Stevie B., Chicago, Illinois. Don't worry, he'll get it.

Just to be sure I grab the attention of all you skimmers, here is *Belushi's Third Rule to Climb Up from Rock Bottom:*

3. TALK TO YOUR BUDDIES.

There are other differences between *my* basic training and the real one at Camp Poodleepoo [Insert name. Thanks, Simone—JB]. For starters, in this basic training program, you're allowed to talk about how you feel.

Now, don't panic. I promise I'm not getting touchy-feely on you. I'm making sense here. When you're out with your buddies, it's okay to talk about how you feel. You may open yourself up to loads of ridicule and potential ass-whuppings, but that's the point. The purpose of your buddies is not just to listen; it's to keep you from doing something stupid. It's to kick your ass if you reach for the phone to call what's-her-name. It's to pound into your skull the news that we've all been there before, that nothing is insurmountable, and that being on your own does not mean you're alone.

Women will ask if your friends all have to be men. Can't there be a chick thrown in there, too? My answer to this question is this: Are you out of your goddamn mind?! Of course you can't confide in a woman this way. They're influenced by the romantic and dramatic much more than men. If you ask a woman whether or not you should go back to your ex and propose to her, she's going to say, "Yes, go! Seize the day!"

Plus, if you go on and on to a woman about your fears, you're never going to be able to get her into bed at a later date. Even if you do, you'll never be able to keep her because you'll have freaked her out. This is important to remember when it comes time for you to start a real relationship with a woman (something you're woefully unequipped for right now). Revealing fear to a woman scares her. Show your fears and wounds to a man, and you have a brother. Show your wounds to a woman, and you have a mother. And unless you're some sicko, or your mother is Britney Spears, you don't ever want to sleep with your mother. The thing is, men know what it's like to be a man. Women don't. That's why you need guys to listen to your shit.

Telling your friends everything that's going on in your head keeps you from doing things alone. For the record, being shit-faced drunk is a completely acceptable and actually preferable way to handle spilling out your innermost thoughts to other men. It brings honesty from both sides, and it's a whole lot more fun. This dovetails nicely into *Belushi's Fourth Rule to Climb Up from Rock Bottom:*

4. BEER IS ALSO YOUR FRIEND.

Beer does not judge you. Drinking lots of it makes you more sociable and funny. You can drink it all night without getting as drunk as you would on single malt. There are many different varieties. Beer can be consumed in a can, a bottle or a frosty mug, depending on the look you are going for and the speed at which you are drinking. Its effect makes women a helluva lot more attractive at two in the morning. And, coolest of all, it's Clint's favorite beverage.

Belushi's Fifth Rule to Climb Up from Rock Bottom:

5. WHEN IN DOUBT, COMPETE.

Men love and excel at competition. It drives us in our work, it drives us in our pleasure. This dates back thousands of years to caveman times. I know this because, despite what you may think, I am an educated man, well-versed on matters of ancient history, especially on a social, cultural and anthropological scale. In fact, there's an episode of *The Flintstones* that backs me up. It's the one when Fred and Barney are bowling . . . Ah, I'm sure you've seen it.

Competition is in our blood. So, when you are hanging out with friends and you get sick of talking, pick up some darts and start playing a buddy (be careful if you are drunk). Grab a basketball and get a five-on-five scrimmage going. (This will help you sweat out all that beer that you consumed in rule 4.) Or—and this would be my choice—go talk up some hot chick you see across the bar (again, be careful if you're drunk). Competition doesn't get any fiercer than when you're competing against every other guy in the bar for a girl's phone number.

Don't be a wuss. So what if you fail? Strength is in the attempt. Think how alive, how secure, you'll feel when you finally get that number. And then the next one. And then the next one. Just be confident and think of this book as the world's greatest wing man. It was either Stevie B. or Abraham Lincoln who said, "The best way to get over a woman is to come over a woman." It must have been Lincoln; there's a reason they called him "The Rail Splitter."

Men need a community. We all need a group of like-minded people who think the way we do, who will distract us from the harmful, and who will uncondition-ally accept us in our darkest times. And it's in that cama-raderie, that distraction and that acceptance where we will learn confidence, security and, above all, how to take care of ourselves.

Hey, we know women share in a community. They have scrabble clubs, book clubs, birthday clubs, char-ity events, girls' night out and yoga classes. And it's a very strong community. How do we know? Because Oprah is so goddamn rich.

CHAPTER FOUR

SUBJECTS ALL MEN MUST BE VERSED IN

Get off my ladder woman, I got to climb up to the top
I said get off my ladder woman, I got to climb up to the top
Get off my ladder woman, ladder's nothing to make you stop

—"Get Out of My Life," Allen Toussaint

So you've found your boys. These boys are different from your "boys," which I can only assume you've found long before this, probably sometime around age two. But you didn't understand their importance until kindergarten, when you encountered a hallowed rite of passage all men must experience: The First Kick in the Nuts. Chances are pretty good that the kick came from a little girl. Chances are even greater that it established a long-term pattern in your life. Sometimes the kicks were real. Other times, they're metaphorical kicks, like a lawyer saying, "Congratulations, Mr. Belushi. Your divorce is final. Again." I digress, but the point is you have to protect your boys just like you have to protect your "boys."

One time my boys and I found ourselves in a bar in Hamtramck, Michigan, dressed head-to-toe in Bears clothing, an hour or so after they beat the Lions on a last-second field goal to keep Detroit out of the playoffs. Paul waved down a bartender and asked in a loud voice, "So are Lions *fans* pussies, too, or just the actual Detroit Lions?" And then—and THEN—when the crowd starts to move in on him—he's the shortest guy in our group, by the way—he turns around, points at *me* and says, "Back off, man. I'm with a celebrity!" (That line alone shows how drunk he was, because this was during my straight-to-video period.)

I look around for Stevie B., but he's walking out the door with some chick on his arm. We weren't in that bar for more than thirty seconds, and Stevie B. has already sealed the deal. (We found him the next day across the river in Windsor, Canada, after receiving a phone call from the border patrol.)

Keep in mind that we're all wearing Bears gear in the Polish section of Detroit, which is a dumb idea to start with. So I look around, survey the angry crowd and say, "Yes, I am. What kind of celebrity? A celebrity who would like to buy everyone in this bar a drink!"

The longest two seconds of silence in my life. And then . . .

Cheers. Backs are slapped, hands are shaken and booze starts to flow. Paul, overcome with emotion, gives me a big hug—at which point I gently remove his wallet from his back pocket.

After everyone in the bar gets their free drink, I hand Paul's credit card over to the bartender. He looks at the name, then looks back up at me and says, "This isn't your credit card, is it?"

I simply remove five twenty-dollar bills from Paul's wallet, hand them to the bartender and say, "It is now."

Five minutes and an eight-hundred-dollar bar bill later (not including an unusually generous gratuity), we're safely on our way.

Using this as a case study, let's take a look at what happened. To put it bluntly, Paul fucked up (big surprise). But I protected him. No punches were exchanged, and no one was hurt. I might not have known him very well, and he might have deserved to get his ass beat, but that night he was one of my boys. So I protected him, because that's what you do. You protect your boys. If you happen to charge $1,200 to keep them out of the Intensive Care Unit of Henry Ford Hospital in Detroit . . . hey, those are the breaks.

You also need your boys to be connected to you. They're there to help you. But they can't do that if they don't have accurate information. So lying to the boys about where you've been, what you've done or who you've done is a giant red flag. You've either done something very, very wrong, or you're about to. Never, ever, *ever* lie to the boys.

The boys are the single most valuable resource you have at this point on your journey back to manhood. So, above all else, you need to treat them with respect. To put it bluntly, that means you need to find something other than your ex-girlfriend to talk about, so they don't toss your sorry ass out of the team after a day.

Lenny Bruce used to say that for every seven years of a relationship, it takes two to kick. But that doesn't mean that you get a year to whine about your ex for every three and a half years you dated. No way. Your ex wasn't a chemical that physically changed your body. She was just some chick. She was skinnier, prettier and smarter than some, but fatter, uglier and dumber than others.

What's that, you say? Yours was different? She was the one you bought Ben & Jerry's at 2:00 a.m. from the cute little corner store, then the two of you went home and laughed and laughed all night, and made sweet, oh-so-tender love down by the fire? Well, she may have been that at one time. But guess what she is now? She's either the Chick You Got Sick Of, or The Bitch Who Dumped You. And if she was eating Ben & Jerry's at 2:00 a.m., she was on her way to being fat. In any case, here's one thing that she definitely is: Gone. So get over it.

Here's what you get with the boys when you get dumped: Two conversations. One to get everything out on the table. Get drunk, get emotional, get in touch with your feelings, whatever. Let it all come out. All the good stories ("Dude, we once had sex nine times in one night. Nine times!"), all the bad stories ("Remember that time I got in the middle of that fight between her and her mother and ended up in the ER?"), and all the made-up stories ("Dude, we once had sex nine times in one night. Nine times!"). There's no time limit on this one. It's like the Senate, they can't cut off debate. If the bar closes before you're done, go back to someone's house. But once you're done, that first conversation, like your relationship, is over.

The second conversation goes like this:

YOUR GUY: "Hey, how are you doing with everything?"
YOU: "Pretty good, I guess."
YOUR GUY: "Yeah?"
YOU: "I think so."
YOUR GUY: "That's good."

That's the second one, and you're done.

It's time to take the next step on your road to reclaiming your place at the table of manhood. It's time for you to become an expert on something, and not only because it will give you something besides your ex to talk about.

And here's my point: All real men are experts at something. So it's time for you to become one. An expert, that is. (Although if you're still reading this book, you're much, much closer to becoming a real man than you think you are.) So pick an area—the more obscure, the better, because eventually you'll be able to win bar bets and drink for free.

For instance, take my area of expertise: Albania. Every time I walk into a bar, I do so with the full confidence that I know more about Albania than anyone else in the room. (Assuming, of course, that it's not a bar *in* Albania.) The good thing about being the world's foremost barroom expert on

Albania is that in the unlikely event that I don't know something, I can just make stuff up. Who the hell is going to challenge me? Enver Hoxa? (You know, Enver Hoxa, the paranoid Communist dictator who ruled Albania with an iron fist from 1944 until his death in 1985.) Luckily, because I know everything there is to know about Albania, I rarely have to make anything up.

[Simone, check on spelling of Enver Hoxa. I'll sound smarter if I throw in as many names of world leader–type guys as I can—JB].

Don't be discouraged by the fact that I've taken up the best area of barroom expertise. There are several other critical ones:

MEAT. Not only do you have to spend more time with your boys at this period, you have to spend less time with chicks. If that ever becomes a problem, here's a trick that will get any woman to glaze over in boredom and walk away from you: Talk about meat.

Let's say you're out with the boys and a woman somehow makes it past your wingmen and into the no-fly zone. Let's even say that out of all the other men at the table, she zeroes in on you, naturally, because of the commanding aura of confidence you're giving off as you deliver your lecture on your newfound area of expertise. Let's say she comes right up to you and says, "I'm sorry. I just *have* to know what you are talking about, and I need to know right now."

You reply, "I'm talking about meat. Where different meats come from. The best kind of meats. The best way to eat them. And how to prevent that pool of blood from forming when a rare steak sits on the platter too long."

I guarantee you, no woman wants to hear that much about meat. Unless she's a chef, in which case she's more of a man than you'll ever be. Trust me, my father and my uncle both owned restaurants while I was growing up, and those kitchens were not nice places. The women in there were tough. They used to chew tobacco while they cooked. They also chewed tobacco while they smoked, which always seemed excessive at the time—and still does, for that matter.

Here's an interesting fact about meat to get you started: There is a "Cattleman's Ball" every year in Nebraska. Not a "party." Not a "dance." Not even a "gala." A "ball." A "Cattleman's Ball." I'm not sure if you actually have to be a cattleman to attend, but I'll bet the food is pretty good.

WAR. Guys like war. We just do. We like pretty much everything about war—except actually being in one, though some guys don't even mind that. War combines everything we all really like—big, noisy machines; good guys and bad guys; winners and losers; screw-ups and great victories. I say this as someone who has never fought in any type of major war, unless you count my teenage years. Although they definitely involved armed conflict, they fell short of true war. It was more of a police action, really.

The good thing about war is that there are plenty of them to choose from. So instead of trying to be an expert on warfare in general, pick one. And again, the more obscure, the better.

I, for instance, am an expert on Albanian warfare. Albanian warfare is different from other types of warfare because, from what I can tell, it means the nonviolent seizure of lands no one ever really wanted. I mean, let's be honest; no one has ever been really excited to invade Albania. There's just not a lot going on. So Albanian military history pretty much consists of ancient Albanians sticking a flag into a rocky hilltop and screaming, "Ours!" while the rest of Europe shrugged and said, "Um . . . okay," and commenced trying to wipe out each other. It's actually not such a bad strategy.

SPORTS. Guys like sports for the same reasons we like wars: winners and losers, Mike Ditka, heroes and goats, Mike Ditka, great victories and stunning losses, and Mike Ditka. The problem with picking sports as your area of barroom expertise is that you have a lot of competition. In fact, unless you are already an expert on sports (and by that I mean someone who makes a living, or has made a living, playing, coaching or covering some kind of major sport), it's too late to start now.

Sort of.

First things first. Just to exist as a guy in the world, you need some peripheral knowledge. You must thumb through the sports pages and know who's in first place in each division; which owner, depending on the season—the Redskins' Dan Snyder, the Mavericks' Mark Cuban or the Yankees' George Steinbrenner—is getting shellacked in the press; and whether or not it's an Olympic year.

At some point, you'll also have to face the golf dilemma. I'm not a golfer, but I can't knock the game. It's so purposeful; you are planting a ball in a hole. And it gave us *Caddyshack*. But following professional golf is different. You really need to be stoned to watch it on TV, so you should decide whether or not you are interested in playing, watching, both or neither, and stick to your convictions. You must never take to the links if you can't play, or talk about the PGA Tour unless you can effortlessly come up with lines like "Vijay Singh laid up just beyond the bunker and he's eyeing a birdie."

The thing is, you have to learn to pick your battles when it comes to sports. Again, to use myself as an example, I am certainly no expert on football. Sure, I can follow the game perfectly well. But on the finer points, such as what exactly constitutes offensive holding, I'm a little murky. My general rule of thumb on holding is that if the Bears are on offense, there is no offensive holding. If the Bears are on defense, every offensive lineman is holding every defensive lineman, and every linebacker and (somehow) two Bears assistant coaches on every play. That's what I know about holding. Which is why, when it comes to football trivia, I have narrowed my "sphere of influence" to just the 1985 Chicago Bears, arguably the greatest team in the history of the NFL.

(I say "arguably" because there are a few old-timers in Chicago who claim that the 1940 Bears, who beat the Redskins 73–0 in the NFL Championship game, were a better team. That debate could, obviously, generate volumes upon volumes of fascinating, in-depth discussion. So I will be reasonable and refer to the 1985 Bears as "arguably" the greatest team in NFL history, until everyone alive in 1940 is dead. I'm talking to you, Joe Dybas!)

Obviously, I'm not the only one who is a barroom expert on the 1985 Chicago Bears. Not by a long shot. In fact, according to the U.S. Census, there are approximately 6 million people who know everything there is to know about the 1985 Chicago Bears. Those 6 million people are also known as "the entire population of the Greater Chicagoland Area."

In Chicago, the Bears didn't win the Super Bowl twenty years ago, they won yesterday. In Chicago, January 1986 was last month. In Chicago, Mike Ditka is still stalking the sidelines, Mike Singletary is still roaming the field, and the "Fridge" is still rushing for short-yardage touchdowns.

In Chicago, Walter Payton is still alive and holds the NFL rushing record. Eat that, Emmitt!

So I don't really care if the New England Patriots have won three Super Bowls in the last four years. In Chicago, they're 0–1 lifetime against the Bears when it counts. In Chicago, they just got their asses kicked 46–10. In Chicago, they got beat so badly they had to change their uniforms.

TELEVISION. Again, it's just too vast a topic for you to become an expert on. Pick one show, track down as many old episodes as you can on cable, and become an instant expert. Stake out your position and refuse to back down.

—"With the exception of *According to Jim*, *Magnum PI* is the greatest television show in history."

—"There is no question that the best years of *Saturday Night Live* were the Belushi years—the Jim Belushi years. Those, and the John Belushi years."

—"I don't care what you say, Don Knotts is the finest actor of his or any generation. The finest actor who is not named Belushi, that is."

You can adjust accordingly, but you get the point.

And as I said before, once you've deemed yourself an expert in your chosen field, don't ever back down. To anyone. It's a good idea to start practicing this skill for later on, when you are married and you really need it.

MOVIES. The following is a list of five movies that are crucial to your development as a real man:

1. *About Last Night*

2. *The Principal*

3. *Red Heat*

4. *K-9*

5. *Curly Sue*

The following is a list of the next five movies you need to watch, learn and love at this stage of your development as a real man:

6. *Fight Club*. Brad Pitt helps Ed Norton strip away all the plastic, useless, bullshit layers of his life, and they get

down to what male bonding really is—punching each other in the face over and over and over again. This movie has it all—rites of passage, secret initiation rituals, smart, subversive humor. And lots and lots of guys punching each other in the face.

7. *The Edge.* Two guys out in the woods, fighting a bear. I'll say it again, with italics, *two guys out in the woods, fighting a bear,* in a movie written by David Mamet, who knows a thing or two about men. But really, if I have to sell you on this movie with any more than "two guys out in the woods fighting a bear," you need to return to page 1, retake the quiz and start this whole process all over again.

8. *Miller's Crossing.* Gabriel Byrne stands alone! He starts off by sleeping with his boss's girlfriend, and it all goes downhill from there. At the end, right when he's about to get his whole life back and everything can go back to being how it was, his boss says, "Well, dammit, Tom, I forgive you!" Byrne's response: "I didn't ask for it and I don't want it. Goodbye, Leo." Because real men don't apologize.

9. *Big Trouble in Little China.* Follow me on this one. Kurt Russell pursues Kim Cattrall throughout the course of this movie. She rebuffs him, looks down on him, holds him up for public ridicule. But then, right at the end, after Kurt has saved the day, she changes her mind. Kurt's

response? Essentially, he tells her to fuck off. This is the only movie I can think of where the male lead tells the female lead to go fuck herself at the end.

10. *Gone With The Wind.* Oh. Right. I guess there are two movies. Technically, Clark Gable said "I don't give a damn," but that's only because no one said "fuck" until Henry Ford invented cars. "Fuck! Why won't my fucking car start?!"

KNOWING "A GUY." Every group of friends has a guy who has a guy. Need a good plumber? Stevie B. has a guy. Reliable mechanic? Call Stevie B., he'll set you up with his guy. Need someone to drive a package down to Miami Beach one day, no questions asked? Steve B. knows a guy, but it's gonna cost you.

Now, you can also try to do things yourself like plumbing to prove you are not a total wuss, but you have to be careful. A buddy of mine was with his new girlfriend when the toilet started to overflow. It was the first time she had been to his house, and he wanted to show her how handy he was. He pulled out a plumbing snake and tried to unclog the pipes. After going in about ten feet, he pulled the snake out, and attached to it by their strings were a dozen or so tampons—some *other* girl's tampons.

To make sure you always have fresh information for your boys, go out of your way to meet some guys who know stuff you don't know. For example, I know how a carburetor works. And somewhere outside of Cleveland, there's a mechanic who not only knows the name of Enver Hoxa's hometown, but also how to say, "Oh, yeah? Well, fuck you!" in Albanian.

If you can't come up with an area of expertise, at least have a story to tell. Something from your own life. I'll give you an example, and I guarantee you that mine beats yours.

The Bulls won their first World Championship in Los Angeles and I was at the game. What a fucking night! What a victory! I had to get down into that locker room and join the celebration. I figured that if I acted like I was supposed to be going there, then no one would question me. Sure enough, a forceful nod was all I needed to breeze right past security into the catacombs of the arena. But for the life of me, I didn't know where to go next. I couldn't ask directions for fear of being ejected, so I walked, full of purpose, through the underground passageways until I found an official-looking, unlocked door. Unfortunately, it was a side bathroom. Rather than look like an amateur, I took a piss and decided to wait it out while the Bulls celebrated next door.

Then the door opened and Michael Fucking Jordan walks in. No shit. The 6'6" guard from North Carolina and his dad had ducked into the bathroom for a private moment—a moment that was now witnessed by me, a two-hundred-fifty-pound lug from Southern Illinois University. (Go Salukis!) No. 23 looked at me and said, "Belushi! We did it!" And as he grabbed my head like he was palming a basketball and gave me an all-star nuggie, he said, "I bet they're going nuts in Chicago!" Me, elated: "Yes! Yes, they are, Mike!" Then he escorted me past security and into the locker room celebration.

Finally, you will need some simple wisdom, some universal human truths that will make you seem wise and interesting beyond your years. I call these bar-bet winners. Here's a few to get you started:

—Why does a doctor tell you to turn your head and cough during a physical? Answer: So you don't cough on him.

—You're on a date, and you're stuck in the bathroom. You've just washed your hands, but there are no paper towels and no toilet paper. What do you do? Answer: Use your socks.

—The mosquito and the crane fly are the only insects that do not have two sets of wings.

—Contrary to Trivial Pursuit, the toilet was not invented by Thomas Crapper. It was invented by Sir John Harrington, a godson of Queen Elizabeth.

And, of course: The dog's name in *K-9* was Jerry Lee, played by Rondo.

CHAPTER FIVE

PREPARING FOR BATTLE

Never Say Die When You Put Me To The Test
The Last Laugh Is Still The Best
You'd Sleep With The Devil
To Get What You (I) Want
Now You See Me Baby Now You Don't

—"Now You See Me, Now You Don't," Glen Clark

Stop reading. I mean it. Put the book down. Wait! Mark your place in the book and then put it down. I hate having to search for my place in a book. Tear a square of toilet paper off and stick it between the pages. (Yes, I know you're reading this in the crapper, but I'm not offended.)

Have you put the book down? Good. Now, take your left hand and pat yourself on the back. I guess, maybe I should've written that sentence before you put the book down, but you probably figured it out by yourself. You know why?

Because you're a man, damn it! You do manly things . . . like pat yourself on the back whilst taking a dump. That's right, I wrote "whilst." We're heading uptown now because it's time to learn about women.

You've already learned valuable lessons that have made you more of a man. In fact, I would not be a bit surprised if your testes have actually swelled since beginning this book. Feel free to check, but please wash your hands before returning to the book. Or you can just pat yourself on the back again, because that shirt is already headed for the cleaners.

The point is, you've changed your outlook. No longer are you a baby sucking at the tit of acceptance by others. You've found a way to complete yourself. To be okay with being okay. Christ, that sounds like something Dr. Phil would say. Let's say it like this: You're now okay with other people not being okay with you, because *you're* okay with yourself.

But it's not enough, is it? Although you've become more than you've ever imagined you were capable of, a nagging emptiness remains in your life. I don't mean the emptiness is nagging you; I mean no one is nagging you, and you miss it. In short, there's a 36-22-36–shaped hole in your heart.

You want a woman.

Note that I said "want." The old you "needed" a woman. The new you "wants" a woman. This is a very exciting moment in any man's life. Most of us start to "need" a woman around age thirteen. But to "want" a woman is a milestone. It means you are being guided by your cerebellum (your "noggin") and not your vas deferens (your "nut tubes").

But now the real work begins. Our journey so far has been all about setting you right. In a sense, this is quite simple, because there's no one to screw it up other than you. Remember when you discovered "sex"? It was fun and exciting and new, and it basically occupied most of your thinking, right? Then it grew stale and you started trying to figure out ways to have sex with another person. It became much more complicated, right? Sex now took more than finding three spare minutes and a bathroom with a lock.

The same is true with self-improvement. Sure, you've laid a foundation to become a new man, but now you must leave the house and expose it to the earthquakes and floods of the real world. And, just like losing your virginity, that's going to mean dealing with women. As you are already well aware, women have remarkable properties that can turn even the tidiest world upside down—properties men will never have, like emotional strength, adaptability and verbal acrobatics. In a very real way, all the work you've done until now has just been a warmup. You've been suiting up in the locker room, and now it's time for you to get in the game. But before you do that, you need to understand your opponent.

What do Napoleon at Waterloo, the British generals in the American Revolution, the Roman legions hunting down Hannibal, the American High Command planning against Vietnam, and Johnny Depp in the first *Nightmare on Elm Street* all have in common? They all got their guts ripped out and handed to them. Why? They all underestimated their opponents. Our opponent: women.

When dealing with women, all we have is the battle. We must abandon any hope that we will eventually win the war. They are too strong. They are too fast. They are too wily. Most Indian tribes are run by women. The tribe appoints a male chief, but the board of trustees are all women. Why? Because women are smarter than men. That's right, they are smarter than us. They can multitask. They are able to give birth, for Christ's sake. That's a life and death experience which takes them to a whole other plane. And most amazing of all, they understand relationships. They created the game, you're just bringing the ball(s).

Abandon any hope that you will eventually win the war. There will be no Knute Rockne speech to inspire you; James Bond will not find the right gadget to escape before the laser saws him in half; Khrushchev will not blink before JFK starts raining atom bombs down on Castro; *Apollo 13* won't safely reenter the atmosphere; and Neo will never figure out that there is no spoon.

This is how it will happen. You will stick your toe in the dating pool. You'll meet a number of beautiful women and sleep with many of them. Eventually you'll settle on one. She'll smell the blood in the water and begin probing for your buttons. And she'll find them, and exploit them, and then you'll drown.

Make no mistake about this—these women will kill you. It's what they do. They say what doesn't kill you makes you stronger. Bullshit! What doesn't kill you makes you bitter.

Have you ever had your heart checked? It's called a stress test. Your heart keeps you alive. Stress is bad for your heart. Name one thing in your life that causes more stress than women. Your job doesn't count, because you're there to make money to keep some woman happy. Maybe not even a woman you've met yet, but be honest. You only have that job so you don't have to tell girls in the bar you're unemployed.

Women stress us out. We stress out about how to find a woman, how to keep a woman, how to dump a woman. Women cajole us into buying things to make our lives easier, then they're on us to keep those things clean, in order and up-to-date. They even stress us out about keeping our heart healthy by not eating too much meat. And then they stress us out about going to get a stress test to see how healthy our heart is.

In truth, they take better care of us than we do. But there's something about this behavior that sets us on edge. So little by little, day by day, they kill us. Don't get angry about it. Simply put, that's why we have women. To slowly, but certainly, end our lives. They are the irresistible force and we are the extremely movable object.

This is not to say that your situation is hopeless. True, over a long enough timeline, you will lose. But it's how you lose that defines your character. Remember *Rocky* (the first one, not the other nine)? The sold-out crowd at the Philadelphia Spectrum is on its feet, chanting "Rock-y, Rock-y!" The date is July 4, 1976, and while Rocky Balboa would not go on to defeat Apollo Creed, the way he lost placed his name on a list of men who shall be remembered for eternity. You see, Rocky knew going in that he was going to lose. The game became about staying in the ring until the final bell—going the distance to prove to himself and all the palookas that he wasn't no bum from down on the docks. And in that final shot when Adrian leaps into Rocky's arms, you just know he may not have won, but he's sure as hell getting laid.

That, gentlemen, is all any of us can ask.

Because you are not Rocky, you will need help fighting the enemy or you will never get laid. And you will certainly never find a wife. There are a few critical things you need to know (but cannot learn from any of Woody Allen's movies—except maybe the one where he plays a robot) so that you won't underestimate women.

Critical Thing #1 That Cannot Be Found in a Woody Allen Movie: You must form your own opinions about women.

Much of what we think we know about women is actually propaganda developed by women. This is not some evil coup designed to hide the truth from us. They honestly believe their propaganda is true. But as is so often the case, they're completely wrong and unable to admit it.

A great example of this is the popular and persistent myth that women are a minority. First of all, it's not true. They outnumber us. We're only about 48.9% of the population. I know it doesn't sound like much of a difference, but try playing some eleven-on-ten football and see how long it takes before you're getting your ass kicked.

The propaganda machine allows for the fact that they outnumber us. We are told that while women are not "technically" a minority, they have historically been "marginalized" and "minimized," suffering many of the same plights of minorities. Sure, but they also want us to believe there is no Bigfoot. Both of those theories are bald-faced lies.

I'll explore the Bigfoot myth in my next book, but for right now, let's look at this silly notion that women have somehow been held back throughout humankind's evolution by the cruel vicious forces of big, bad, smelly man.

Most of the so-called intellectuals who believe that women have been oppressed point to the fact that it wasn't until 1920 that the United States gave women the right to vote. The suffrage movement gave rise to the feminist movement. I am not an opponent of the feminist movement; I just haven't been excited about any of their positions since they advocated women not wear bras. Had that edict been in place when I was a teenager, it would've saved me countless hours of trying to figure out how to undo a triple clasper. I'd go so far as to say I'd endorse any political movement that advocates less underwear.

Consider this. In 1920, before women could vote, the average life span of an American male was 53.6 years. Horrifying for this fifty-year-old author to consider, but nonetheless true, according to whatever web site Simone found the statistic on. At the same time, the average life span for an American female was 54.6 years.

Right there should be a huge red flag. The poor, put-upon women toiled without a political voice for the first 140-some years of our nation's history, but yet they are winning on the most important scoreboard there is—life. As "bad" as they had it, they still got an extra year.

There are lots of reasons to explain why men don't live as long as women. Our average life spans are skewed by men who die early because of war, working dangerous jobs, or from our innate curiosity about explosives. The equalizer in this equation is childbirth, which has yet to kill any men, at least not directly. Yet even though we were "in charge," we took these risks and paid the price by living shorter lives.

By 1995—seventy-five years after the whatever-number Amendment [Simone, I'm sure you know, but please double-check—JB] gave women the right to vote was ratified—the average life span for men was 72.9. That's pretty damn good, if your idea of a good life is outliving your prostate. For women the average life span, however, has increased to 79.9. So instead of outliving us by one year, they outlive us by seven.

How do women have the gall to say that women's health initiatives are underfunded? Damn right we should be studying women's health. For starters, I'd like to see a study about why the hell they are going to live *seven* more years than me. That's a long time. By age seven I could already tie my shoes, shuffle a deck of cards and pee into a urinal thirteen feet away. Think of what we could do with that time at the end of our lives. And what does the National Organization for Men have to say about it? Oh, right, there is no National Organization for Men. Because we are not considered a minority.

Why is no one screaming from the rooftops about this? Women have taken their political clout and used it to live longer and longer, while systematically killing us. The numbers back me up here, but you've never heard this theory before, have you? You know why? It has been censored. Women don't want you to think about this stuff and see how they're holding us down. So they keep it out of the media . . . which they control. And when's the first time you hear it? In a book by Jim Fucking Belushi! A sitcom actor! They think you aren't going to take me seriously. They think you'll assume I'm a crackpot. Well, I'll cop to being an actor, but I'm no crackpot, and when you read my book about how Bigfoot shot JFK, you'll know it's true.

Let's look at that whole "women finally won the right to vote" thing. Think about American HERstory up until 1920.

Driven by religious persecution and the nagging of their wives, men come to the New World and settle in the harshest of conditions to forge a new nation. Eventually, because of economic persecution and the nagging of their wives, our forefathers shrugged off the yoke of monarchy and created a new nation. Driven by the quest for natural resources and the nagging of our wives, we expanded the boundaries of our country from the Atlantic to the Pacific. After much bloodshed and nagging by our wives, we finally deal with the issue of slavery. Slowly, we became less agrarian and more industrial, and our economy became increasingly self-sufficient. (I don't really understand this last sentence, but I copied it off my desk mate during a history exam in eleventh grade and it stuck.)

In 1917, the war in Europe and the nagging of our wives became too much for us and we sent troops over to kick some German ass. We came out on top in World War I and finally the chant "USA #1!" had some teeth to it. At this point, we came into our own as a nation and truly became a world power.

Then what happens as soon as we're on top of the world? Women want to vote. Right away. No waiting. Like that friend who shows up for the fourth quarter of the game and steals your last slice of pizza. I hate that guy.

But we are America. So we give them the vote.

And what happens? Prohibition. The Depression. Hiroshima and Nagasaki. The Cold War. Television starts rotting our brains. The Bay of Pigs. The Cuban Missile Crisis. The Vietnam War. Kent State. The Cubs blow an eight-game lead to the Mets. The Saudi oil embargo. Watergate. The Iranian hostage crisis. Love Canal. Three Mile Island. Double-digit inflation. Reagan gets shot. The Shuttle tragedy. AIDS. Crack. The Bears fire Ditka. North Korea gets the bomb. Jordan retires. And let's not forget: Oprah is on TV every single day.

Heck, practically the only thing in America that hasn't gone right down the crapper since 1920 is the Augusta National Golf Club.

Have you ever heard the argument that the fact that no woman has ever been President of the United States is proof that they are being repressed? That's more propaganda. All they have to do is run a woman, and they should win. I mean, there are more women than men, and the last time I checked, the person with the most votes at the end of the day becomes president. Unless, of course, you are Al Gore.

The point is, women don't want that job. No, I'm not some patronizing chauvinist who doesn't think a woman could hack it as president. I'm saying they don't *want* the job because they've seen the videotape. Every president is sworn into office apple-cheeked and full of energy. Within six months his hair is white, his face is cracked with age, his shoulders slump, and his blood pressure has risen twenty points.

If you read the Constitution, the first thing a woman would have to do when she runs for president is admit that she's at least thirty-five years old. Then, if she is elected, the stress is going to age her ten years. What woman wants that job? Besides, they don't need it. They already run things.

This goes to the core of the issue of women working. Did you ever notice that if a woman has a kid and then goes back to work, she's "trying to have it all"? No one ever asks a guy if he's going back to the office after he has a kid. A woman stays home to raise her children, and she's a "mother." A man does the same thing and he's "unemployed."

And, by the way, only in the past fifty years or so has anyone really wanted to go to work. If you look at history, for 99% of the population, going to work meant *work*: Mine shafts with no ventilation, steel mills, the blazing heat of wheat fields, lumber mills with saws that can cut your nose off before you can sneeze. It sucked. It's barely been a hundred years since we really had a work day that wasn't all day. Going to work meant sweating, struggling and sometimes dying. Believe me, I know. I'm an actor. I've had to play guys like that.

Sure, there are now more "white collar" jobs that can promote creativity and satisfy people's ego, but that's pretty much a brand new idea. I mean it's recent. As recent as, say . . . the feminist movement lobbying for women to be taken seriously as part of the "work" force.

Obviously, I'm exaggerating. I mean, if I actually believed some of the things I had written above, then . . . well, I'd never get laid again. So don't go quoting me on any of that. It was just for your amusement. Laughing helps the action of the colon.

My point is that we've been brought up to think that women need our help, that we're holding them back, and that we need to be gentlemen. Guess what? It turns out that "gentle" and "men" are antonyms. (That means "opposite." Use your noggins, you nut tubes.) All I ask is that you don't underestimate women. Remember your Clint? Use it. Women are an opponent. Don't think that they're frail and weak beings who are recovering from the shitty hand history dealt them. You know who thought that about his opponent? Custer. Do you know what Custer's last words were when he saw Sitting Bull and ten billion Indians riding down on his men? "We're fucked."

Don't be Custer.

Be Rocky.

Critical Thing #2 That Cannot Be Found in a Woody Allen Movie: Men like to subtract, women like to add.

Remember seeing that footage of the "spider hole" they found Saddam Hussein hiding in? He was buried under a hut with a single light bulb, some rudimentary plumbing and about $750K. Now, if you're anything like me—and you're getting more so every time you turn the page—you had one thought about the "spider hole": If it gets cable, I'll move in tomorrow.

This is the nature of man. We have few needs. We must eat, we must sleep, we must crap, we must watch sports. Everything else is gravy. Oh, I almost forgot that one. We *need* gravy.

Don't be confused. Sometimes you think sex is a necessity, but ask any thirteen-year-old boy and he'll tell you there are many ways to accomplish what you "need" out of sex. Compare Saddam to Imelda Marcos. Did Imelda hide in a spider hole? No, because chicks don't go into spider holes. They found Imelda guarding her two thousand pairs of shoes.

Women add. Men subtract.

If you told a woman she had to live in a spider hole, the first thing she'd do is decide what color to paint the walls. Undoubtedly, it would be one of those many shades between periwinkle and cornfeather. Next she'd figure out a way to get some sunlight, which would, of course, necessitate window treatments. Before you know it, she's thinking of adding on so she can have some closet space, and complaining that you never entertain in your spider hole.

It's just the way things work. Remember those cave paintings they found in France? Chicks did that. Guys don't sit around figuring out what to put on their walls. If they found porno on the walls, then I'd wonder if maybe it was a guy, but it was just pretty pictures. Smells like a chick to me.

Here's an example of chick math. Say a girl and a guy each put on five pounds. What does the guy do? Probably nothing. I mean five pounds? That could be gone with one good Sunday afternoon in the john. The truth is, a man won't really do anything about his weight until his pants get too tight. Most of us would just wedge ourselves into the pants and hope the problem goes away. But we know that might cut off circulation to the boys. Instead, we go buy fat pants and resolve to lose weight. So for men, weight gain is only a problem because it means we have to go shopping. It's also a problem with a solution, and men are good with solutions.

A woman discovers weight gain *while* shopping. She's really a size eight, but they have the cutest dress and the color she wants is only available in a size six. So she squeezes into it, and while she zips up the back she feels the cellulite squirming for freedom.

Right there you see the dichotomy. Men want to lose weight so that they can own fewer clothes. Women want to own more clothing. The only common ground in weight gain is that both sexes worry that getting fat could mean that no one will ever want to see them naked again.

Let's say a man has to lose weight. What does he do? He starts to work out. He mixes in a salad every now and then (whenever he's not eating with other guys) and switches to light beer (also when not with other guys).

How does a woman lose weight? She goes on a diet. She reasons, "I can't fit into a size six, so I must not eat for three months."

"Hold on a minute," you say. "Isn't that a case of men adding and women subtracting?" Correct. That's also the first time you've caught me contradicting myself since you started reading.

This is not the example that spoils the rule. It's true the woman "subtracted" food, but consider what she will have to "add" to continue the diet.

Eventually, she will be eating in a restaurant and will have to consider the menu handed her by the waiter. Men like menus. It's as if someone took the universe of all the things to eat and condensed it into a simple two-page, laminated list (preferably with pictures).

But women see menus as a good starting point. A

woman will spend twenty minutes reading a menu, deciding what she "should" eat instead of what she "wants" to eat. A guy takes thirty seconds. The only real question is whether we want our dead cow served to us ground up on a bun with cheese, or as a slab with a baked potato. If a woman is on a diet, then deciding what to order for dinner starts shortly after breakfast.

The formula is complex and arcane. It involves a chart of her caloric intake over the past seven days. Grams of fat and carbohydrates are calculated; sugar and sodium totals are considered. Eventually she'll order lettuce with light dressing on the side, but arriving at that conclusion may take hours. And that's just the brain power she uses when it's actually time to eat. When she's not eating, a woman becomes obsessed with all things edible. She'll start talking out loud about whether or not she can afford to eat a snack, the status of her diet, how much weight she's lost or gained. When a woman walks up the stairs, she wonders how many calories she's burned. A man walking up the stairs wonders when the hell the elevator will be fixed.

So she may have subtracted food, but in reality, she has added a project for herself—trying to figure out how to reconfigure the menu so she can eat dinner and still lose weight at the same time. She'll ask the waiter, "Could you please have the chef use white wine vinegar instead of red wine, leave out the pearl onions and put the dressing on the side, but make sure it has no-fat canola oil instead of vegetable oil as its base." Guys don't do that. We work out, do our best on the salads, and when we can fit into our old pants without cramping our junk, we're done.

Critical Thing #3 That Cannot Be Found in a Woody Allen Movie: Women overcomplicate and men oversimplify.

When I was living with one of my first two wives (but before I married her), I was driving home alone one afternoon when out of the corner of my eye I spotted a banner on the local sports bar trumpeting "Quarter Wing Night." My reptilian brain did some calculating and weighed the relative merits of cheap chicken wings, beer, and sports, versus going home to see my "lover." Before I could even process this thought consciously, my car was pulling into the parking lot.

This is classic male oversimplification: meat +beer + sports +cheap =good.

I finally made it home several hours later. Before I could remove my keys from the lock, my future-alimony-check-recipient was all over me, angrily asking where I'd been, what I was thinking and what was wrong with me that I didn't call. Didn't I value the relationship? Wasn't this relationship going anywhere? And when the hell were we going to get married?

This is an experience men refer to as the Pearl Harbor Phenomenon. It's an unprovoked attack that comes without warning and is virtually impossible to defend against. Often this is attributed to "hormones." In truth, however, what happened was neither unprovoked nor unexpected. (You like how I did the neither/nor thing? I almost sound like Frasier now.) While I had oversimplified things to the point of sucking down beers and wiping bleu cheese off my chin, my future-alimony-check-recipient was at home furiously overcomplicating things.

Women like to know what's going on. At all times. No, they don't only want to know, they want to "nose." Why? Because they're nosy. It's how they remain in control. Of everything. No less than three times that day, I had received phone calls from my future-alimony-check-recipient. To me, these were simple, if perhaps a bit irritating, "How you doing?" exchanges. To her, these were high-priority communiqués to be dissected with more detail than German U-Boat transmissions. When she casually asked what time I thought I'd be home and I answered "the usual time," my future-alimony-check-recipient had assumed that I was focused on the conversation, not on beating my high score on Minesweeper.

Five minutes after my expected return home, my future-alimony-check-recipient began overcomplicating things. First, she assumed I must have been stuck in traffic and felt sympathy for me. Fifteen minutes after my scheduled arrival time, she began to suspect that I had stopped to buy flowers to surprise her. Certainly I had given her absolutely no evidence to believe this would be the case, but since I said I'd be home "at the usual time," what other explanation could there be? With each passing minute my future-alimony-check-recipient's glee blossomed like the flowers that would shortly be in her hands. By thirty minutes past the appointed time, however, suspicions darkened.

Thirty minutes, she knew, was enough time for me to go through foreplay, sex and a nap. Now she began to wonder if I was having a rendezvous that night. But with whom? A girl he works with? An ex? One of her friends? That bitch Maryann! She knew she couldn't trust her around her man.

She contemplated packing her bags and leaving, then decided it would be more prudent to chuck all my belongings out the window. Reaching into my underwear drawer, she paused when she saw the boxers she'd neatly folded and the socks she'd paired. She wondered what I would do without her. It was now an hour past when I was supposed to be home. And standing there, staring at my underwear, my future-alimony-check-recipient realized how much she'd miss me. This brought a wave of sadness. She remembered what it was she loved about me and realized that I couldn't cheat on her . . . even if that whore Maryann would be all too happy to jump on me if she turned her back for even a minute.

Immediately, her sadness turned to fear. Something had happened. I said I'd be home by now. If I wasn't here, it meant something terrible had happened.

So while I was sitting in a bar watching the seventh inning of a baseball game, my future-alimony-check-recipient reached the inescapable conclusion that I must be lying in a ditch somewhere, brutally mangled by a horrific car accident. For the next hour she wondered whether she could love a man confined to a wheelchair, or a vegetable who needed a machine to breathe for him. What if I was dead?

She systematically called all the local hospitals and morgues, who all have special hotline numbers for hysterical women—all of which she had memorized.

By the time I crossed the threshold of the front door, it was as if a ghost had darkened her door. She was elated and relieved until she spied a dab of wing sauce on my collar. At that moment, it would actually have been better for me to have walked in with Maryann on my arm.

What I had done wrong was ignore the fact that man invented the cellular phone expressly for this purpose. Sure, if you're stranded at the South Pole, they come in handy, but the main function of a cell phone is for men to call women to tell them where they are. Obviously the tertiary use is for women to tell men that what they are doing is stupid, and they should come home, and pick up some milk on their way.

In fact, most inventions throughout history have been created for this dynamic. Necessity is the mother of invention, and mothers are the mother of necessity. The wheel came about so that men could carry more shit back to their wives more quickly. Locks were invented so that women would have something to wake their men from a dead sleep to go "check." The telegraph was invented so that men in the Western frontier wouldn't be immune from the inquiry of "When are you coming home?" The light bulb was invented so that men could illuminate a room in the middle of the night, proving that there were no spiders present. The Internet was invented so that men could be pretending to check sports scores, when in reality they are just one click away from lesbianfantasies.com.

The fight I walked into was inevitable because women overcomplicate and men oversimplify. I forgot to look at it from the women's perspective. It's a perspective where things like chicken wings and Kerry Wood starting against the Cardinals pale to the likes of a long discussion about all the permutations of what could have happened to me on a drive home if I don't use the cell phone to call and say I'll be arriving late.

Critical Thing #4 That Cannot Be Found in a Woody Allen Movie: Remember that you don't think like a female.

Porn is actually a great example. Yeah, I was still thinking about it from two paragraphs ago. You too? It is a beautiful thing. You know why we think like that? We're men. We like to think about sex, we like to have sex, and we like to watch sex—a man and a woman having sex, a man and two women having sex, a woman and four midgets having sex, pretty much anything having sex as long as a woman is in the mix.

Men like things to be easy. If you hooked up with a character from a porn film—note I didn't say a porn star; I'm talking about a "character" from the movies—then you'd never have to worry about sexual urges again, because there'd be a chick even hornier than you. It would be a chance for you to subtract sex from your list of things to worry about.

Women don't like most porn because some of it portrays

women as being powerless. Women only like porn when it's dressed up and presented as a French art film. These films have beautiful people making love, not lesbians in a 69. The films are shot in the French Riviera, not a seedy motel. And they have romantic music over the sex scenes, not chicks saying "Oh, I hope that pizza came with extra meat."

Women want a man who will ravish them while whispering how much he feels for her during the experience. Even if they found the equivalent of a porno character, they would need to add things to the man to make him a complete package.

Just look at a newsstand and inspect the rows and rows of porn. Hey, if anyone catches you there, now you can say I sent you. See 'em? You can probably do this from memory. *Jugs, Beaver Hunt, Shaved, Barely Legal, Black Tail, Jerk Off to This!* You see that and wonder where you'll find the time to peruse it all. Women look at that and say, "Why does the world need eighteen magazines that are exactly the same?"

Women hate all this porn, but turn your head and you see *Brides, Modern Bride, More Brides, The Knot, So You're Getting Married.* You want a million dollar idea? Start publishing a magazine called *Dirty Nude Brides.* You'll have the highest circulation ever. [Simone, copyright that. That's the little "c" in the circle.—JB.]

Women think differently than we do. This is hardly news. Hell, Oprah says that. So you know it's not even one of those truisms they keep secret to trip us up. No, this is out there in the open. That's one difference right there.

They *never* forget that we think differently; we do the forgetting. We want to believe that they "get" us and they're "simpatico." Forget about it.

They not only know we think different—they think that the way we think is wrong. The implication, of course, is that the way they think is correct. Who hasn't stared down the barrel of that loaded gun?

Sure, she understands there's a football game on. She gets that it's the playoffs and they're . . . important. But football's on every weekend. And they play the playoffs every year. But today is the only day that area rugs are on sale at IKEA, and you agreed that you need a rug for the den, and . . . couldn't you just . . . tape the game? There's another invention. VCRs were invented so wives could tell us we could just tape the game. As if it doesn't matter that it's happening live. Ugh, just thinking about it hurts.

But they keep at it and pretty soon you start thinking that you don't get it. After all, it is just the Wild Card game, not the Conference Championships. And she's right; you do need a rug. Pretty soon she's undermined your manliness. You start questioning whether you know anything at all. That has to stop. You've worked too damn hard to figure out what kind of man you want to be.

Don't let them decide what's important to you. **Always remember that to a woman the *relationship* is more important than you are.** You have to know in your heart what you want. Make a decision and then stick to it. Be forceful like Clint. Don't be swayed when she's upset that you'd rather stay in and watch *The Bridge on the River Kwai* for the fifteenth time rather than go out for sushi with Stu and Marcy. You don't like sushi (except with cheese on it). You don't like "couple time." Hell, you don't even really like people. You just want to be in a spider hole, remember? Let her be content in knowing that for the next three hours, you'll be sitting with a beer and some bad sausage and at least she'll know exactly where you are. This is the attitude you have to take once you start interacting with women again.

Now that I've scared the shit out of you, let's go get one.

BOOK TWO

★

DATING, ACCORDING TO JIM

CHAPTER SIX

ARE YOU READY TO DATE?
TAKE THIS SIMPLE QUIZ

I Travel From Maine To Mexico
Just To Find A Little Girl That'll Love Me So
No Matter When, No Matter Where I'll Be
Lookin' For A Woman That'll Satisfy Me
Have Love, Ow ow Baby
I Will Travel
Have Love, Woo Baby
I Will Travel
I Said If You Need Lovin' Then—Hmmm
I'll Travel
Hmmm, Baby
I'll Travel

—"Have Love Will Travel," Richard Berry

Today, my friend, is your lucky day. Congratulations.

Now, don't go running off to the racetrack with your last two paychecks in your pocket quite yet. Wait, you know what? Maybe you should. What the hell—you've earned it. If you've made it this far, then you deserve a break. A pat on the back or a pat on the front, if you can get one. So grab your cash, hit the track, and go win some money. I'll be here when you get back.

Hey! Welcome back. How'd you do? If it really was your lucky day, then you're rich and this is the only dating advice you're ever going to need again:

Open your wallet.

Like Stevie B. always says, when it comes to attracting women, "You gotta have it HERE, or you gotta have it HERE." (It makes a lot more sense when you can actually see Stevie B. first pointing to his wallet and then to his crotch.) If you've got money, you've got women—because money means status, and women love status. They love money too, because it means they can buy more shoes.

But if you didn't win any money, or if you actually lost a fair amount of cash . . . well, that's too bad for you. Guess you'll have to wait for my guide on how to play the ponies to be published [Simone, just write down "Real Men Bet the Trifecta"—I'll know what it means—JB]. But, today is still your lucky day. Just not at the track.

In fact, today is a such a lucky, red-letter day for you that even the scratch you just blew down at Santa Anita doesn't outweigh the good fortune you're about to receive. Today is your lucky day because I'm going to give you the one, simple, all-inclusive rule for successful dating. If you do nothing else but follow this one rule, you absolutely cannot fail when you finally hit the dating scene again. And that rule is as follows:

You're not ready.

Hey, man, that's fine. You don't have to believe me. Frankly, I wouldn't believe me if I were you, either. But if you're so confident that you're ready to just dive dick-first into the singles scene, then I'm sure you don't mind proving it to me by taking this simple quiz about what you're looking for in a woman and what you're offering her. One point for each correct answer (beware of deductions), and don't forget to keep score.

1. You see a sexy woman across the bar, and she sees you. Do you:
   a) Challenge her to darts, pool or whatever bar game you have mastered; stakes are winner gets a blow job?
   b) Look away quickly before she sees you're interested, tell your buddies this chick is giving you the eye and keep finding excuses to not talk to her until she leaves?
   c) Yell at her to stand up on the bar so you can see how big her ass is before you walk all the way over there?
   d) Send her a drink, walk over and introduce yourself and trust your charm and personality to get you somewhere?

If you are Antonio Banderas d) will work, but if not, you're going to waste a lot of time. If you answered "tell her to stand on the bar and show her ass," you'd better be on spring break, because any woman with that low self-esteem, you don't want to wake up with. No points for this answer—unless you are actually on spring break. The answer I like is a) because you're doing what you would normally do, and if she agrees to blow you if you beat her at pool, then you two will probably get along well. Even better, you're being sexual right up front, so if you hit on her later, she has no room to complain.

2. First date. You've finished small talk, cracked a joke, broken the tension. She starts to talk. The first important words out of her mouth will be:
   a) "I'm not that hungry. Want to fuck?"
   b) "So I should probably get the STD thing out of the way . . ."
   c) The Lie.
   d) "You remind me so much of my brother."

The correct answer is c). I have a big chunk of this section devoted to it. Trust me, it's right. Take away a point for any other answer, because you don't date women who say any of those things on the first date!

3. You're halfway through your first date with a

woman when another man asks for her phone number right in front of you. You . . .

a) Grab the nearest fork, scream, "I've got a number for ya, pal!" then show him the number of prongs on the fork, scream, "Four!" and plunge it into his eye socket. She will think you are strong and decisive. So will the other guy.

b) Do nothing. It's really about her reaction.

c) Smile and say, "Take my phone number too, 'cause that's where she's waking up."

d) Get up and leave. Any woman who gives another man "come and get my number" signals on a first date will be cheating on you within a week.

The correct answer is c). It shows her that you're confident and in control of the environment.

4. You're planning your third date with her, and the first two went well. You can expect:

a) Sex.

b) Anal sex.

c) Her to cook.

d) All of the above.

If you said "anal sex," she's a hooker. Sorry. If you said "all of the above," then you obviously have all the answers, so where's *your* book? The answer is c), and hopefully it will be a cheeseburger with a side order of sex.

5. You've been dating for two months. She looks around your place one day and says, "You know what this place needs?" How do you respond?

   a) You stop listening and begin planning your breakup speech.

   b) You turn off the TV and listen intently. This is half the reason you got a girlfriend in the first place, isn't it?

   c) No response at all. She can have this conversation without you.

   d) You turn off the TV and listen intently, because she is secretly telling you what is wrong with YOU, disguised as telling you what is wrong with the apartment, to soften the blow.

In a relationship, this is just the sort of out-of-nowhere shit you are going to have to deal with, so give yourself a point for any answer, for good luck. Remember, she is a woman. You will never know why she says these things, so be grateful for the sex and cooking.

6. You've been dating one girl for about six months, when you meet another girl at a party. You talk all night, she's great, and she gives you her number

without your even asking. The first girl finds the number the next day. How do you play it?

a) "That? That's not mine. Call if you don't believe me."

b) "That? Oh yeah, that's this guy Suzanne. I told you about him. He's having trouble with his homemade Go-Cart, and I'm supposed to help him out today."

c) "What the hell did I tell you about touching my stuff?!"

d) "Yeah, some girl shoved that in my pocket last night. Jealous?"

The answer is d). You're a man with options. She should know that. It keeps her intrigued.

7. You've known a girl for a couple of years. You've done things together a lot, as friends, but you want it to go to the next level. You:

a) Rent a couple of Jon Cryer movies from the eighties, cook her dinner and make your move.

b) Get her drunk and make your move.

c) Just grab her and kiss her spontaneously, hoping she mistakes your complete lack of cool for sincere, guileless passion.

d) Realize that you are her friend, you will never be anything BUT her friend, unless you do something stupid like grab her and kiss her or get her drunk and make a move, in which case, you're just a sad, weasely asshole.

If you responded with anything except d), then clear your schedule, call in sick, and READ THIS BOOK!

8. You are meeting her friends for the first time at a party. You know nobody there but her. You:
   a) Stick close to her, follow her lead, be charming and make them all like you. The message is, you're a couple.
   b) Flirt with her girlfriends, disagree vigorously with her guy friends, find out who has banged her and start a fight.
   c) Behave exactly as you would if you were there alone, but make out with her in the corner at every opportunity.
   d) Be cool, distant, aloof. Let no one know what you're thinking. Leave early "to go to this other thing."

These are all varying degrees of right (or wrong). To earn the point, you need to have selected the most right answer, which is c) because all she really wants is for people to know you're really into her. The runner-up (sorry, no points) would be to go to that other thing because it never hurts to be mysterious, and all her friends will be talking about you when you leave (which is why you leave early). See?

9. You've been dating a woman for about six months. You've recently begun to suspect that she may be cheating on you. What's your course of action?

   a) Confront her. If she admits it's true, dump her. If she denies it, stay together.
   b) Confront her. If she admits the affair, ask her if it's another woman. If it is, ask her if you can join in. If she denies it, stay together.
   c) Find a way to work it out no matter what. If you've been together that long, there must be something important. At least, important enough to try and forget the image of some other guy's tongue in your girlfriend's mouth.
   d) Confront her. If she admits to it, dump her. If she denies it, still dump her.

Here's a little truism I've come up with: If you think she's cheating on you, then she is—and she'll never admit it until the day she dies. So the only possible answer is d). (However, take away one point for not checking to see if it was another girl for a possible three-way.)

10. You have just had sex with her for the first time. The first words out of your mouth are:

a) "Is it cool if I wipe my dick on the pillowcase?"

b) "Wow. Had I known you were that good, I would've let you order the lobster!"

c) "I love you. I mean that sincerely . . . at this particular moment in time."

d) "Well, it's getting late. Maybe I'll call you or something."

This is the most important question on the Dating Quiz, and if you answered any of the above, you lose all your points. Whether it's a one-night stand or the love of your life, you just SHUT UP! I can't stress this enough. She will place enormous importance on whatever you say after the first time, and no matter what it is, it'll be the wrong thing. Shut up, let her talk, stroke her hair, and do not get up to take a leak. Let her leave the bed first. Speak only in response to a direct question, and once you have answered it, SHUT UP!

Time for the scoring:

You got the last one wrong. Don't try to dodge it. That wiped out all your points, which means you need to read the following "Dating" section all at once, in a quiet place with no distractions, which should be easy since you're probably single and there's no football on today. Wait! There's football on? What the hell is wrong with you?

If you scored below zero, then you are obviously not ready to start dating. You may not even be ready to start talking to women. (Notice I said "start." If you score this low, there's a strong chance you have yet to actually see, much less speak to, a woman.)

Not counting the final question, if you scored anywhere from 1 to 11, you're doing a little better. In fact, you can probably start dating right away. You'll be fine. Even if you're not, I'm sure the women you date will let you know when you're doing something wrong. And I'm sure you'll follow their advice—just about dating at first, then about the clothes you wear, the food you eat and how to spend every waking minute of your life. In six months, they'll be telling you which hand to hold your dick with when you're in the bathroom. But that won't matter six months after that, because by then you'll be sitting down to pee. And in two years, you'll be right back at the beginning of this book.

Sorry, but you're not ready to date. That, my friend, means you need to keep reading.

CHAPTER SEVEN

HOW TO GET A PHONE NUMBER

All You Pretty Women You Gotta Take A Chance
Half The Fun Of Livin' Is Doing The Dance
Sixteen Men Standing All Alone
Looking For Somebody To Call Their Own
Can't Get Out Of It
Can't Get Out Of It
Can't Get Out Of It
You Might As Well Get Into It

—"Can't Get Out of It," Glen Clark

My wife, Jenny, is the most beautiful woman on earth. The fact that I am crazy in love with her notwithstanding, she's seriously hot as shit. I'd go so far as to say that if I took her to a bar and asked five guys if they thought she was hot, they'd all say "Hell yes, what's she's doing with you?" But that would mean five fistfights and five lawsuits and my lawyer insists on charging me separately for each suit.

There are two reasons I mention Jenny's beauty here. The first is, she's going to read this book, and I'm not above kissing my wife's ass in a blatant attempt to get even more sexual favors than I'm used to. The second is because I need to talk about another woman. A woman that I would otherwise describe as the most beautiful woman on earth . . . were it not for the fact that I'm currently married to the woman who so clearly holds that title. That would be my wife, Jenny, the most beautiful woman on earth.

The *other* woman's name was Chloe. Think about it, have you ever met a woman named Chloe who wasn't hot? This girl lived up to the name. In fact, she was so hot she could have lived up to the name Svetlana. But her name was Chloe, and she was (at the time!) the most beautiful woman I had ever seen.

Obviously, this was before I met my wife, Jenny, the most beautiful woman in the world. In fact, it was shortly after I had been put through boot camp by Stevie B. and my boys. I had learned my terms and the tools I needed to stay true to them, so Stevie B. told me my Jedi training was complete and I was allowed to go out and hunt for a mate.

Not a day later I met Chloe. I was doing a photo shoot, and she was one of the people organizing it. She was (at the time!) the most striking woman I'd ever seen. Gorgeous face, tall lean body, and buckets of attitude. Everything about Chloe said "Don't approach me, I am too good for you." She was cold and officious. Every guy on the set was flirting with her, and she responded only in sneers and icy stares.

The old puppy-dog, rock-bottom Jim wouldn't have looked twice at Chloe—she was too hot. Old Jim would have assumed she'd never be interested in him. Old Jim would instead look around the studio and find the fat catering girl. Old Jim would buy the fat catering girl a diamond necklace to get her to go out with him, date her for six months, propose to get her to sleep with him, and then give her half his shit when they got divorced. Old Jim was such a pussy, and really fucking expensive to keep around.

But Chloe wasn't meeting Old Jim. She was meeting New Jim. Better than New Jim, she was meeting New Jim *on a mission.* And when I greeted her, I was locked on target.

I pursued Chloe. Once I got to know her, I realized she was the type of woman who used to destroy me: smart, strong-willed and bossy. The type that for me was like a bad cold that I could never get rid of. My Clint was going to get a workout. Was I up for this? My Curly and my Gandhi were solid, but my Clint was my weakest. It scared me, but I knew this was the perfect woman to test out my new skills. Like Clint says, "Do you feel lucky, punk?"

I did feel lucky. And it turns out my newly developed skills worked even better than advertised. I melted Chloe's chilly exterior. In fact, she became a warm, giggly schoolgirl who would sit by the phone waiting for me to call. And let me just say this about my time with Chloe: Whoa. Were I not currently married to the most beautiful woman on the planet, I would say that was the best sex I ever had.

Going after the hottest woman in the room was a marked

improvement from my old *modus operandi*. Actually getting her to acknowledge me and go out with me was nothing short of a miracle, considering the guy I used to be. But the real achievement here was I managed to *not* marry her and therefore *divorce* her.

Jealous? You should be. Because you aren't there yet. You think I forgot about your sad performance on that quiz? Because I did the work in Book One, I was able to be the type of man who would attract Chloe. But Chloe couldn't know that until I got her attention. How did I get her attention, you ask? Hmmm, it just so happens that Book Two is dedicated exclusively to this subject. I'm going to take the new you from the barroom to the bedroom.

I know you just found out you aren't ready to date yet, but you should feel really good about yourself. And you will! Provided you don't screw it up now. And you will! Because men always screw up! How do I know this? Because, my friend, I have the scars, restraining orders, and alimony payments to prove it. You must accept that you will screw up. I had Stevie B. to walk me through it, and you, my friend, have this book.

So how do you meet a girl out and about in the real world? Where's the best place to do it? When you see a good-looking chick, how do you know if you should approach her? What should your first line be? How do you chat her up after that? How long should you talk to her? And, most importantly, how do you get her phone number?

Now please keep in mind that there was a time in my life when I had absolutely no skills when it came to picking up women—and none in searching for the right mate, which is what you are really doing.

What we're about to jump into is a list of skills that you need to practice. It's like free-throw shooting in basketball, or learning your lines when you're about to do a movie. You have to practice in order to be good. Practice makes perfect.

Let's start from the beginning. Let's start with someone who has no idea how to meet a girl. Let's start with that whiny, pathetic, insecure little weasel in all of us. In short, let's start once again with Paul.

Paul is so scared about being inferior to all the other men out there, and most of the women, that he won't put himself out in public. He stays home, waiting for the phone to ring. In other words, he resorts to the *passive* role in male-female relationships—the female role, the role designed for the person who waits at the bar for the man to come up to them. And that's not a role a man wants to be in.

We're active beasts. We didn't wait for the T-Rexes or Triceratops to come kick the shit out of us. No, we went out of the cave to go after them. We hunted them down, killed them, cooked them over an open flame and then mounted their heads over our cave fireplaces. Believe me, unless my sources are wrong on this, those goddamn things made good eatin'. Why do you think they're extinct? Asteroid, my ass.

You're far enough into these pages to know what Paul is lacking. "Balls" is one answer, but I think we can be a little more specific. The poor jerk lacks poise—the poise to be who he is and be accepted, as well as the confidence that he can be someone he *isn't* and still be accepted. This is a quality I've referred to in earlier pages. This is a quality that both Paul and you will need. To get started you must:

1. Find a place where you're both comfortable.

Where's the best place to go to meet a woman? Well, first off, you're wrong to think there is a single best place to go. You can meet them anywhere. Why? Because they are everywhere. For some reason, women tend to believe it's their right to go wherever they please. Don't ask me why. I wasn't one of those dudes who signed the Constitution. If I was, then I would've made the whole process much easier. For example, these days, if you want a carton of milk, you go to the supermarket and buy a carton of milk. Why couldn't it have been like that with women? If you wanted a woman, you would go to a store to buy one. Think how easy that would be!

Where you meet women isn't that important, provided you meet them in a place where they are comfortable. If they're comfortable, they're more at ease. They can let their guard down. And this is the best time to work. A party thrown by friends is a good example of a comfortable atmosphere. A deserted parking garage would be a bad example.

Now that we've got "where" down, maybe it'll help if I get a little specific and focus on one location. Let's say the "where" is a birthday party thrown by a friend of yours. And let's say the party is being held at a bar somewhere near your house—a bar you know pretty well, a bar whose booths you've cried in and bathrooms you've thrown up in many, many times. Let's say she feels comfortable here, too, because it's a neighborhood joint.

So, gentlemen, let me be the first to say . . . Welcome to O'Drinky's!!

Paul steps into O'Drinky's, and who does he immediately notice but this blonde sitting at the bar. She is a birthday party guest, but Paul has never met her before. Great, right? Paul seems to be sitting pretty. He's in a place where his confidence and her comfort should be high. So what's stopping him from going up to the girl and talking to her?

His lack of balls, yes. I think it's safe to say that any question I ask pertaining to Paul can be answered with a comment about him lacking a set. So, from now on, let's consider any question I pose to you about him as rhetorical.

I'll tell you what Paul's problem is—and this is a problem that ails many men. They are not sure whether or not the woman is interested. Paul has no idea what to look for, what feminine signals to be aware of or not aware of. He must:

2. Notice the "shopping" signs—the man is the product.

Think about it. What do women know better than men? Yes, relationships. But what is number two on that list? Shopping. Women know shopping like men know . . . well, *not* shopping. Shopping is in their blood. They're programmed at birth. They have shopping so deeply ingrained in their systems, they can tell if they like something immediately after seeing it.

Next time you're shopping with a woman, look at the expression on her face when she sees something she likes in a store window or a display. Her face lights up. She can't stop looking at it. She gets giddy. She'll find any way to pick it up or touch it. For those of you out there who have never been shopping with a member of the opposite sex before, take my word for it, this is how a chick reacts.

In the great big shopping mall that is the male-female relationship, Paul is the thing the woman wants to obtain. See, at this stage of the game, it's okay if you, the man, think of yourself as a product. Her first instinct is to take you home with her. But first she needs to look at you, touch you, feel you, smell you and price you. Now, naturally, there's a lot of bullshit that happens in a woman's mind after that initial reaction to keep you from getting laid, but nevertheless the reaction is still there. You just have to notice it.

She smiles at you. She establishes eye contact with you from across the room. (Make sure there isn't a clock or a TV over your head that she is looking at instead of you. This will save you untold embarrassment.) She moves into your personal space. She touches you. Some women just touch everyone, so you can't read into that. But if a woman touches you casually more than once—it's a sign that she likes you and you better pick up on it. At this point, you need to check for a wedding ring (third finger not counting the thumb, left hand).

Okay, let's say that Paul is getting these signals from the blonde sitting at the corner of the bar. They're subtle and infrequent, but if Paul knows what to look for, he can definitely see they're there. So she likes him. She wants to talk to him. What's next? Go up to her, right?

Wrong! First, it's important for Paul to see if *he* likes her. Does *he* want to talk to (or, more realistically speaking, sleep with) her? For women, that's an incredibly complicated question. Luckily, for men it's usually simple:

3. Ugly = Bad / Pretty = Good.

This sounds easy enough, but let me just say up front that it doesn't always hold true. If you are on the rebound or desperate, shoot low. If your confidence is low and there are five hot chicks and one mediocre one, go for the mediocre one. For one thing, there's less competition. Besides, you know the old saying, "There's something beautiful about every woman." You should find what's beautiful about her and focus on that. The opposite applies when you break up with a girl—find what's not beautiful about her and focus on *that.*

Even when shooting low, you need to be careful. You need to know your territory. In college, a buddy of mine was desperate one night. He had taken a swing at every chick who walked into his sight line. It was last call, creeping up on 2:00 a.m., and he had been shot down twenty times. After being literally swept out on the curb by the bar's staff, he found himself next to a woman who was overweight and plagued with chronic acne. She was also into that punk thing and had short, badly dyed hair and a nose ring. She smelled like cigarettes and booze. My buddy was so hammered that he didn't know the difference.

Desperately horny, he starts chatting her up. Pretty soon they're making out right on the curb. They somehow stumble back to her place and they have wild sex. Finally, they both pass out.

The next morning, he wakes up and looks beside him. Lying there is this frighteningly ugly beast. Slobber is dripping from her snoring mouth, and her doughy ass is hanging off the side of the bed. He grabs his pants and heads for the door. He's just inches from a clean getaway when she wakes up and tells him it was "fun." He gives her the obligatory "I'll call you" and splits. He walks out her front door and realizes that she lives . . . RIGHT ACROSS THE STREET FROM HIM.

Let's cut Paul a break and say the girl that he's pursuing at O'Drinky's is a knockout. So now he should go up to her, right? Almost. There's one more thing to look for—a drink in her hand. Ah, yes, liquor. Our oldest friend. Always there when we need it; often there when we don't.

Well, right now we need it. If you see a girl who intrigues you, it's essential that the girl be drinking something alcoholic. One, the effects of her drink will instantly make you more handsome, more interesting and much funnier. Face it, this broad's not gonna laugh at your lame Yakov Smirnoff impression unless she's good and loaded. Two, because it lowers the lovely lady's inhibitions and makes her feel more comfortable—lest we forget that's what we're going for in the first place. Let's call this an amendment to my previous rule:

3a. Girl + Booze = Friendly Girl

Now, in this case, the Happy Hour special at O'Drinky's is white wine. Perfect. It's an elegant, thoughtful drink that turns the most elegant, thoughtful lady into a "possibility." Time to move in. But wait, what does Paul say? What's his first line? A warning:

4. Don't resort to opening lines. Simple is better.

First I'm gonna tell you what his first line *shouldn't* be. Here's a list of the five worst first lines in history:

A. "Are you wearing space pants, beautiful? Because your ass is out of this world."

B. "If I could rewrite the alphabet, baby, I'd put 'U' and 'I' together."

C. "That's a great dress, gorgeous. It's gonna look a whole lot better on my bedroom floor."

D. "Do you have a little German in you? Would you like some?"

E. "Hi, I was in *K-9*."

Trust me, I ended with the worst one in the bunch. Opening lines don't work. They never work. And guess what? You never have to use them! Paul can go up to this woman, introduce himself using his *real* name, and *still be cool.*

Okay, so Paul has introduced himself. As he talks to her (and I'm going to bring up what he should talk about in a moment), it's important for him to remember the key word—poise. Portraying CONFIDENCE is essential. Always maintain eye contact; always keep her attention; always position yourself a safe distance from her, not too close yet not too far away; try not to touch her too much or, if you touch her, do it gentlemanly; and never, never get caught staring at her chest. But if you get caught, hope that she is wearing a necklace that you can compliment.

Maybe I'm being a little bit cautious here, but think about it. If you don't adhere to these few simple rules, you'll seem like someone who needs her more than she needs you. And that doesn't keep the woman interested. You'll lose her attention and she'll start looking around O'Drinky's for someone who *will* maintain her intrigue.

Now, what should Paul talk about when he's chatting this chick up? Some guys think that this is the hardest step in this whole gruesome process. But it's not, it's the easiest. There's no trick in getting a woman to talk. Follow the simple equation:

5. Keeping Her Talking = Keeping Her Guessing.

Get *her* to figure out what to say. If Paul's lady is anything like *every other woman in the world,* this won't be a problem. Keeping her talking makes you a great *listener,* as well as making you all that *more mysterious.*

Now, a woman can say one thing and be thinking something completely different. All the better if she shows not just shopping but true buying signs, such as complimenting you, revealing details of her routine, or talking about future activities together.

So, as this girl Paul is talking to is going on and on about her parents or her job or the fact that the Cubs didn't make it to the World Series (if a woman is going on and on about that, by the way, she's the perfect woman and you just jump right to the section in this book about living together), what she's thinking to herself is "Oh, this guy listens so well," and "I wonder what he's *thinking.*" See? She's intrigued. She doesn't know where Paul is coming from exactly, but she wants to find out. He will need to:

6. Keep the conversation just four minutes long.

Of course, because women love to talk and they think you love to listen, something surprising and even sinister tends to happen if the conversation drags on too long: They become overly comfortable. She starts to think of you as a girlfriend instead of as a potential boyfriend or bedmate. That's why when you're talking to a woman for the first time, you have to keep the conversation short. Use the 3:1:4 formula— Ask three questions, answer one, get the number in four minutes, then get out of there. That leaves just enough time for you to seem interested, interesting and mysterious. And that, dear friends, results in a woman who is intrigued—a woman who wants to give you her phone number.

If she outright volunteers her number, you've done it. If she's hinting about getting together, you will need to come out and ask her. Some girls need to be asked—it's all those damn Merchant-Ivory movies they've watched. After the four minutes are up, be simple and brief. Don't beg, just ask. Try something simple and direct. "I'd like to take you out sometime. What's your phone number?"

There are a few big don'ts at this point: Never accept her work number or her e-mail (unless you can write love poems like Wordsworth), and never volunteer *your* phone number. I used to have guys tell me that they've given three girls their number. "What!" I'd say. "Are you the chick? Girls aren't going to call you." All that will happen is that you will end up sitting by the phone, hoping against hope for that call. Sitting around waiting for an e-mail is even worse. You have now become "the chick."

That's it, my friends. That's how you do it. If Paul follows those six simple steps, he'll have no problem meeting a woman and asking for her phone number—and neither will you. Really, that's all you have to do once you've laid the groundwork.

Watch, it's easy:

PAUL: Hey, I had a nice time talking to you. Can I have your home phone number?
GIRL: Sure. It's KLondike-5-6969.

119

See? Simple. I'm not sure why I made her have a phone number from the 1930s, but it adds a little bit of subtext, don't you think? Remember, even if she did give Paul her phone number *out loud,* what she was saying internally was something completely different:

> PAUL: Hey, I had a nice time talking to you. Can I have your home phone number?
> GIRL: Sure. It's KLondike-5-6969. I want you to call me after an appropriate waiting period. Then, after a couple of dates, I'm going to take you back to my apartment and make you my anytime I want jelly-roll.

Girls are cute, aren't they?

But Paul could never be that slick. Despite me pleading with him to stick to these rules, he ignored the four-minute limit and kept chatting the girl up. The four-minute rule is there for two reasons. One is to create romantic mystery. We'll get into that in the next chapter. The other is to keep you from doing something stupid in the spur of the moment. Paul was about to do something stupid.

"You're so easy to talk to, Nicole," Paul enthused, "because you're so smart." Even Paul had learned the number one rule of seduction: "Call the smart ones pretty and the pretty ones smart." Trust me, it works. Because it's something different. Pretty girls always hear how pretty they are, but don't hear "smart" enough. And the smart girls don't get complimented enough on their looks.

Before you know it, Paul had spent the entire night talking to her. It was understandable. After his girlfriend Kate dumped his ass, Paul went so long without feminine contact that the Commission for Male Virginity reviewed his case and declared him a virgin again. Then Paul began flirting with Nicole and he started thinking she could be his slumpbuster.

"Slumpbuster" is a term from former Cub Mark Grace. A slumpbuster is a woman who may not be easy on the eyes, but is . . . well, easy. It brings a hitter's confidence back better than any batting coach or corked bat. For Mark Grace, going three games without having a game-winning RBI is a slump. For Paul, going the entire Clinton administration without getting laid is a slump.

The key to slumpbusters is they should be anonymous. Choosing a coworker, friend or cousin is only going to come back to haunt you. Remember, you're rusty.

But despite all we know about Paul, Nicole actually invites him back to her place. Even Paul knows this is a green light.

The problem is that during the course of the evening, Paul consumed several drinks. Why? Because he was nervous, since the only woman he's spoken to in the last two years is the operator who takes his orders for the J. Crew catalog. Holding a glass gave him something to do with his hands. But by the end of the evening, his bladder was ready to burst.

As they drove to her place, a conversation took place in

Paul's head. Essentially, his nuts and his bladder were arguing over who got to use the penis first. His bladder was saying "I gotta pee! I gotta pee!" and his nuts were saying "I'm going to get laid! I'm going to get laid!"

Despite virtually no contribution from his brain, Paul had to continue to flirt with Nicole until they reached her apartment. Once inside the door, Paul counted to ten so as to create the illusion of casualness before asking, "Can I use your bathroom?"

To which Nicole, still flirting, replied, "No, you can't."

Paul was aware she was flirting, but his bladder answered, "No, I really need the bathroom." Nicole finally agreed to let Paul use the facilities. You know, drain the main vein. (How come you never hear chicks use the phrase "relieve the beav"?)

Soon Paul had not only finally been able to unload his bladder of its terrible burden, but he had also overcome the last obstacle between him and intercourse. Surely now there was no *possible* way Paul could screw up his shot at sex.

Not so fast. Paul cannot say what happened next: It may have been a dual stream issue or a piss shudder. All we know is that Paul's stream made an abrupt right turn and shot down the front of his pants. His tan pants.

I know none of you would ever make the series of mistakes that Paul did resulting in him standing in Nicole's bathroom with a dark stain from his knee to his crotch. But pretend for just a minute that you were that clueless. What would you do?

If it's me, I turn on the faucet, splash water all over my pants and come out of the bathroom fuming, "What the fuck is wrong with your sink?" I'd make *her* figure out a way to make things better. Remember, her insecurities are your leverage.

Another tack would be to take off your pants and every other article of clothing, walk out of the bathroom naked and say, "Why do you still have your clothes on?" The girl only has two choices then: Sleep with you or throw you out. If it's the former, make sure you last at least two hours because you want your pants to be dry when you have to put them back on. If it's the latter, walk out of the apartment immediately with your stack of clothing under your arm. Don't give her the satisfaction of watching you put your clothes back on.

What did Paul do? He exited the bathroom and approached Nicole, who didn't immediately look up. In a loud, clear voice, Paul said, "I've whizzed on myself and I have to go home."

Nicole paused from opening a bottle of wine for the two of them. "What?"

"I've whizzed myself and I have to go home."

Nicole ventured a glance up at his crotch. "Oh."

"Yeah." Then, summoning up what he considered to be all his dignity, Paul moved to the door and opened it.

Just before he left, Nicole offered, "I'll talk to you tomorrow."

Paul considered this. "No you won't," he concluded,

before walking out of the apartment. For the first time in a long time . . . Paul was right.

I tell you this story for two reasons. One, if I ever let Paul live that down, he just might go out and screw up like that again. And two, while Paul may have taken the issue to ludicrous heights, it goes to show you how unprepared you are to go out with women. Sure, you'll do better than Paul, but is that the standard you want to be compared to?

Now go get that number. But remember, be careful out there.

CHAPTER EIGHT

PRETENDING TO BE A LOT MORE INTERESTING THAN YOU REALLY ARE

So you're sneaking and Hiding behind His Back.
And you've got a Man that you don't like.
Put That Cat, Baby, Out of Your Mind.
Follow Me, Honey. We'll have a Real Good Time.
This Is It.
This Is It.
Look What You Get!

—"Three Hundred Pounds of Joy," Howlin' Wolf

You have the Holy Grail: the phone number of a cute girl. So I guess you should get on the phone and call her, right? Wrong! The phone number for a hot girl is like a handgun. There's a cooling off period before you're allowed to use it. Once you get that number, you have to be willing to wait.

Romantic mystery. You remember how important I said

it was to define yourself as a man? Romantic mystery is just as important. As important as it is for you to define yourself to yourself, it's just as important to *not* define yourself to women. The less a woman knows about you, the more she has to fill in the blanks. And she's going to fill in those blanks with what she *wants* you to be. You do not call that woman for three days. You'll become more desirable to her as each day goes by.

How many times has each of us been asked by a woman for the "guys' perspective"? "Ummm . . . can I get the guys' perspective from you? If I gave a guy my phone number and he hasn't called me in three days, what does that mean?"

You try to answer in a way that makes her feel good about herself and subtly cuts off the dude she's asking about at the knees. Not that you believe any of your reasoning. You're just playing friends with her in the hopes that at some point she'll realize she should be sleeping with you. But she won't. She's thinking about that other guy, not you, because he hasn't called her. He created romantic mystery. He let her go through the three stages of anticipation: Wonder. Hope. Need.

Day one of you not calling her is Wonder. You did such a good job getting that number that she's sitting at home wondering if you'll call. "He seemed interested. I *wonder* if he's going to call me."

On Day two, Wonder turns into Hope. On the passion scale, hope is more potent than wonder because it adds the element of self-doubt. "I *hope* he's going to call. I *hope*

I didn't do anything to scare him off. I *hope* he's still interested." And still she waits.

Day three is Need. "Oh, my God. Maybe I'm fat. I wore my ass pants and everything. Was I too desperate in the bar when I gave him my number?" They'll never admit this to their female-empowered girlfriends, but they *need* you to call.

Waiting three days doesn't sound like fun to you? You want instant gratification? Too bad. This is work, my friend. Luckily for you, it will be easier now that you know what kind of man you are, but hold on to that. It's real easy to lose that man after the next three days have passed. Women will drive us crazy. But what sweet insanity it is.

So what work do you still have to do before you call her? Ask yourself, "What's your story? What movie are you giving this woman the opportunity to costar in?"

Your first couple of contacts with a woman is like showing the trailer for a movie. If you edit it right, it'll be a movie she wants to be in. Wanna know why guys in bands get laid so much? Because their movie trailer is exciting and interesting. Women want to be the woman who can get an exciting guy, not the woman who nailed the nerdy guy in accounting.

You wanna know why? Better character. Better story. Better movie. There's a certain type of guy out there who drives women wild. The type of guy women would cheat on their man with in a heartbeat. You know the kind I am talking about: the band guy, a swashbuckler, a cowboy, a domineering CEO of a Fortune 500 company, a gruff-but-lovable everyman with his own show on ABC.

Women say they want a man who is kind, gentle, compassionate, polite, considerate and nurturing. Bullshit! They just described a chick! Women really need a man who is mysterious, powerful, passionate, confident, unpredictable and a little dangerous. That's the guy they will sleep with.

Why not let the woman you're pursuing think you're that guy? Now, I know I wrote earlier that you need to define who you are and never waver from being that person. I still mean that. You need to know who you are. So here's a crazier idea: become that guy.

You have to seem interesting and exciting. Wanna know how to do that? Again, romantic mystery. The most interesting person in the world to a woman is someone they know nothing about. The stuff they come up with in their own head is a lot more interesting than you. It's the same reason you are always a little disappointed the first time you see naked boobs that you have been working like hell to get your hands on; you've created a mystery in your head that is better than real life. But a man who has the guts to walk up to her in a crowded bar, get her number, leave soon afterwards, then not call her for three days, must have one helluva story.

That's why so many women out there have a crush on Tony Soprano. He cheats on his wife, works in an illegal business and kills people. Yet they're drawn to him.

Big Tony's a real guy. A take-charge guy. He's a powerful, dangerous, aggressive and unpredictable guy. He would kill to get what he wants or believes in. And on top of all that, he's a guy who is working to make himself better, but never changes. What woman wouldn't want to be the one to tame that beast? What a movie to be a part of!

When a woman gives out her number, she's hoping you're as exciting as Tony Soprano—the type that turns her on. Don't give her any reason to think differently. And in her mind, you will be that type until you prove her romantic fantasy wrong. Loose lips sink ships. All she needs to know is that you have the Four P's: Poise, Power, Pluck and Put it to Bed.

Poise. You got her number. You have the balls to call her, and the balls to assume she'll remember you after three days. You are confident, cool and collected.

Power. You set the terms. You set the date. She's along for the ride. Sweep her off her feet. This is your movie. She's the costar.

Pluck. Make yourself somewhat unattainable. Show her that she'll have to work for you. In essence, challenge her. Keep her intrigued. If you're too easy, there's nothing for her to try to change or chase.

Put it to Bed. This is more than just about getting a chick in the sack. This is about making decisions and finalizing things.

Okay. You feeling exciting and interesting? Check the calendar. Has it been three days? Are you kidding me? It took you three days to read ten pages? Don't you ever go to the bathroom?

Give her a call. Reached the answering machine, huh?

She's probably screening calls. That's a standard ploy women use to not seem desperate, even though she's sitting and waiting for you to call. *Don't leave a message.* If you leave a message, *she* gets to decide whether or not to call *you* back. And her ego gets satisfied without you getting the date. You want to keep the control. Remember, a man who is in control is sexy.

And let's face it, men sound like idiots when using their sexy voice, and once it's recorded she can play it back to her friends. Plus, we have to sit and *wonder* if we sounded like an idiot, then *hope* we didn't. And eventually we *need* to know if she thinks we sounded like an idiot. Sound familiar? It's because you've made yourself the chick.

Don't leave a message. Make her jump to answer the phone when it rings. Now, because my fan base is an intelligent crafty bunch (and huge RadioShack geeks), you're thinking, "What if she's got caller ID?" Don't worry, kid. You're still aces here. More romantic mystery.

"Oh, my God. A number I don't know. Someone called. I *hope* it was him. I *wonder* if it was. I *need* to call that number right now and find out if it was him, but hang up so I don't look desperate."

By the way, if you get a hang-up call shortly after calling her, wait another three days to call back, just to make your point. You'll get an earful when you do reach her, but that's PLUCK, baby! And it's all really about making her feel *something*. Making sure she's not bored. Inspiring emotion. Men exercise their bodies; women exercise their emotions.

I didn't learn this until after my second marriage, when I was dating Jenny. I slowly created mystery and maintained control by never calling her. I let her call me. One day, she complained, but I was ready.

"It's not fair that you don't call me. I never call men," she said.

"What's wrong, it's not working for you?" I asked. "If I called you a bunch, would that work for you?"

"Yeah . . . yeah," she said.

"Is that how it used to be with the other men in your life?"

"Yeah," she said.

"Did it work for you?" I asked.

"Well, actually, no."

"And this seems to be working," I pointed out.

"Yes . . ."

In general, the less time you spend in contact with her, the more time she spends thinking about you: why you are not in contact with her, what is wrong with her that would make you not contact her, and what she needs to improve to keep you interested when you do contact her. You have become a *challenge*. Advantage, men!

You want this because, believe me, if you do wind up dating this girl, she's going to spend a lot more time thinking about what she needs to improve in *you* to keep you interesting.

So, you're calling her . . . and she picks up! You're all set because you did your homework. Wait, you didn't do your homework? Hang up! You think this is easy? This is a sport, guys. Not soccer, either. A *real* sport. You gotta have a game plan. You need to watch film and prepare. I thought you were farther along that this. You're damn lucky you've got one helluva coach with an extensive playbook. Let's try this again.

Know what night you want to take her out. And by no means can that night be a weekend night. If a woman thinks you don't already have plans on a weekend night, she assumes you do not have anything going on. Pick a weeknight. Monday, Wednesday or Thursday. Not Tuesday. You don't want to miss *According to Jim*. Not Friday or Saturday either. You have better things to do with your weekends until she earns that night. Why should you be the only one who has to prove his worth?

Know where you are going to take her. Lunch, dinner, coffee or a drink is acceptable. Someplace nice, but not too nice. Rule of thumb: If people are there for their anniversary, it's too fancy; if entrees come on a plastic tray, it's not fancy enough. Got it? Good.

Know your game plan. You want to have a pleasant conversation for about four minutes, and then ask her out. Nothing more. You are calling for a date, not to chat. Women don't chat with guys they want to have sex with. They chat with their girlfriends. And women do not sleep with their friends, except for on certain artistic masterpieces on Cinemax.

How do you keep from calling and chatting? Remember

the 3:1:4 formula. Ask three questions. Answer one. Be off the phone in four minutes. It works for getting phone numbers as well as getting dates. Buy a four-minute hourglass timer if you must [Simone, make sure they produce four-minute hourglass timers. If not, contact National Invention Registry. The number is on speed dial.—JB].

Remember, women think we are much more interesting than we actually are. Less is more. Let her do the talking. You and I both know that getting a woman to do the talking ain't gonna be hard. When four minutes hits, ask her out for a specific weeknight.

If she is excited and free on the night you have designated, get her address, tell her politely that you will pick her up at 7:00, and hang up. **Do not** tell her what you're doing in advance, but give her a hint of what to wear. **Do not** have any contact with her until you show up at her doorstep at seven. **Do not** call her to ask if you are still on. **Do not** call her for directions. **Do not** call her to tell her you are on the way. She will want you to call, because it will calm her fears that you'll stand her up. You don't want to calm those fears. They're part of romantic mystery.

Those fears cause her to wonder if you are going to stand her up, hope you aren't going to stand her up, then need you to not stand her up. It stirs up her curiosity (which, as a single man, is your greatest weapon). But as soon as she sees you at her door at 7:00 as you promised, she will be ecstatic that you are there, and her fears will immediately subside. This will make you a hero to her before the date has even started. And she won't care if she's overdressed because she'll just be glad you didn't stand her up.

If she sounds enthusiastic on your four-minute call but isn't free the night you offer, wait for her to make a counteroffer. Do not make one yourself. Listen, I know you want this chick bad but you do not want her to know that, or she will make you work like hell for her. If she thinks you can take her or leave her, she'll work to get you!

If her response on the phone is not enthusiastic, don't beg. Say goodbye and immediately hang up the phone. She's not into you, and you don't need any more friends. You already have your buddies. And don't feel bad about doing it. If she didn't want to go out with you, she shouldn't have given you her number in the first place.

If she just flat-out says no, don't ask for an explanation, don't argue, just get off the phone and go back to square one. Face it. Things wouldn't have worked out—and she's probably a lesbian. The more you hear "no," the easier the lesbian thing is to believe.

Here's a little piece of advice our old friend Stevie B. gave me: Make one of those questions in the first phone conversation, "What's your favorite kind of movie?" If it's romantic comedy, tailor your date to a Hugh Grant movie and your story to a romantic comedy. If it's action-adventure, take her some place action-packed, like a hockey game or a hike in the woods at night. If it's *Mr. Destiny*, propose to her on the spot. If it's an Ingmar Bergman film, she is quietly dangerous (picture her cutting herself with a piece of broken glass), and you don't need this challenge. If it's *The English Patient,* hang up the phone. Now! Before the four minutes are up.

CHAPTER NINE

THE DATE AND ITS POSSIBLE NUCLEAR FALLOUT

I'm The King Of The Road
A Coupe De Ville Is My Throne
As Long As I Got The Dough
I'll Be Goin, Goin, Goin, Goin, Goin, Gone

When It Comes To the Women
I Can Do No Wrong
I Can Wine Them and Dine Them
And Sing Them A Sweet Love Song
*   I'm The Cadillac Man Until All My Money Is Gone*

                        —"Cadillac Man," Glen Clark

This is it. You're on. You may get laid, you may fall in love, you may try to tell an amusing anecdote with something green in your teeth, and you haven't even ordered yet. I can't be there with you to hold your hand and walk you through it in person because I'm busy making television to amuse you on your night off. Besides, you wouldn't want me there, because the chicks really dig me and it's your date. But with a short checklist, you will be ready for that first date.

SHOWING UP

Look good, but not your best. You don't want to be her prom date; it puts too much pressure on the evening. Personally, I don't care what you wear, as long as you don't wear tights. Men do not look good in tights unless they are starring in *The Pirates of Penzance*. Bow ties are stupid, unless you've won a Nobel Prize (and I imagine a number of Nobel laureates are reading this. Who knows? They need something to read in the can too). And the best place for a monogram is nowhere on your clothes.

Here's the thing. Chicks may want a dirty, dirty boy. But they don't want him to look dirty. They want clean. Go easy on the hair gel. Don't ever outdress them. Finally, I'd recommend having one button in the middle of your shirt undone. That will make you look vulnerable and make her feel needed when she fixes it.

I've heard a lot of people say that if you feel comfortable wearing something, then it's appropriate. While this is normally true, it can be a major problem after a breakup of a lengthy relationship where your ex-girlfriend bought all your clothes. A buddy of mine had broken up with a girl he was dating in the nineties and decided to get himself back in the game and out on the town. Not wanting to wear the clothes his girlfriend had bought for him, he put on his old chick-luring clothes and was laughed out of the club when he showed up wearing Hammer pants and a *Miami Vice* jacket.

A word to the wise on *her* clothes: Compliment them. Compliment her hair, and especially her shoes. Women like when you notice their shoes because, from the ankle down, any woman can look like Cindy Crawford. But don't be too specific. My second wife taught me so much about women's clothes that I could identify Manolo Blahnik shoes, Prada handbags and La Perla undergarments. After we divorced, I went on a date with this chick who was wearing all of the preceding, and I casually named them to her. She looked at me and said, "You know way too much." I never got a second date, because I knew all her secrets.

If you know what a woman likes down to the brand of shoes, where is her power? Women need to feel power. You can't be an expert at everything—especially things that are her territory—because it doesn't make her feel needed or special. She has to be powerful in her area and have her secrets because she too has an ego. Come to think of it, I guess I did mention her brand of shoes and the fact that I was in *Pirates of Penzance,* so maybe she just thought I was a big, cross-dressing homo.

And don't try too hard to impress her on the first date. No flowers, no violins, no limousines. You won't have any way to top yourself for a second date. Unless you're not planning on a second date, in which case, why the hell are you shelling out for flowers, violins and limousines?

THE DRIVE

Remember that when you talked to her on the phone, you left her in the dark about where you're going. Mystery. She's going to have a lot of questions about the night's activities. Mystery. She will love the place because it's a surprise. Even if it's Denny's, it'll be cute because it was a surprise. It may even be romantic to her.

THE RESTAURANT

Don't pick a restaurant you have never been to before. Don't pick a restaurant to impress her. Pick a restaurant with good food that isn't too loud. Eat slowly, because if you finish too fast, she will feel rushed. You're going to talk—and by that I mean *she's* going to talk. You're not married yet, so you have to listen. She will ask you questions, then answer them for you, then tell you what she thinks about what you're saying, even though you've said nothing. Nice job.

Think of a date as a job interview. You're deciding if you want to hire her, and what position she might be good for. (You see what I did there with the word "position"?)

The thing is, if you start answering a bunch of questions, she'll be interviewing you. Don't start a big discussion about a movie you might see, and don't ramble. You ask her three questions, you answer one. Then repeat as necessary.

Remember, the first thing a woman says about herself is "the lie." It's what she really wants to be, but isn't. She doesn't know she's lying, it's just human nature. We see ourselves as the ideal person we'd like to believe we are. (Guys do this too.) So if she says, "I hate playing games. I'm not a game player," then obviously she's a huge game player. If she says, "This is the first time I've done this," she's done it before—and she's good at it. Maybe even a pro. If she says she doesn't sleep with guys on the first date, ask for the check. Get her home immediately!

A great line of questioning on your first interview with a woman is to ask her about her father. It's been said that girls look for men that remind them of their fathers. Find out what kind of relationship she had with her dad. She says she didn't see eye to eye with her dad? Be a jerk. Be confrontational, critical, loud and rude. She says her dad was cool and distant? Step back, don't overreact, be stoic and aloof. She says "Dad and I are best friends"? Pay the check and go home. Alone. You aren't ever going to live up to that, so don't even try.

In the rare case where you find a woman who is shy, don't interview her. Buy her a glass of white wine and wait. *Don't you try to fill the silences.* That's her job. Easy, right?

Not really. This is one of the most difficult things in life:

allowing the silences. In music, it's not how much you play during a song, it's when you pause. In acting, it's not how much you talk, it's when you talk. Consider Steve McQueen, the man of all men. He barely spoke. He would look at a scene and give everybody else his lines—as long as he had the last shot of the scene. So if you want to be like Steve McQueen, if you want to come off as Thomas Crown cool, enjoy the silences. And if you are really good, try manufacturing some silences.

When I took Jenny out, she talked the entire date. All I did was listen. Afterward, her girlfriends quizzed her about the lunch (note: lunch, and it was a Wednesday). She told them it went great and that she really enjoyed it. Next, they asked what I was like. She stopped and said, "I have no idea." Mystery! I made her feel heard, which made her feel good. I also created mystery and romantic fantasy, so she wanted to know more about me.

The only questions I asked were along the lines of, "Are you going to eat those fries? What about the other half of that sandwich?" Was I being a pig? No. I was establishing that I was a food stealer. From that point on, she knew her food was also my food. Neat, huh?

THE ACTIVITY

What did you think, a six-dollar plate of potato skins and a glass of house wine was going to have her on her back?

No, you have to go do something with her now. You need to engage in an activity. The standard activity is a movie. I recommend any of the fine Jim Belushi films available on DVD back at your place, assuming you've cleaned the toilet and made your bed.

If your place is messier than you'd like, you can go out to a movie. You pick, but don't make it *Ninjas at Mardi Gras* or some crap she's going to hate. If she suggests something, be careful. If you haven't heard of it, there's a reason—it's about a career-minded girl coming to terms with her mother who's got cancer or something. And it's three hours.

Non–movie activities are fine, but be smart. It's your first date.

GOOD	BAD
A play	A school play
A party at someone's house	A wedding
A basketball game	A poker game
A museum (if you're so inclined)	A roadside gator farm
A short boat ride	A cruise
A bike ride	A bungee jumping contest
A bar	A titty bar

Is it going well?

You will ask yourself this question several times over the course of the evening. Let's define our terms. "Going well" can be defined as "leading to sex," or just plain old "having fun." If it's a long-term thing, you might rephrase it as "leading to a deeper, more meaningful relationship based on mutual respect and affection." Same thing. At the end of the night, is she going to leave your apartment with your respect?

Some signs to watch for: Is she making a lot of eye contact? "Yes" is good. Is she finding reasons to touch you? Ditto. Is she laughing at your jokes? Not too many of these, even if you're funny. She wants a man, not Gallagher.

You are building to Your Move, wherein you close the deal, so it's beneficial to have some rough idea of how Your Move is going to be received. Some women will give you obvious signs that you are clear for launch. This can happen at any point in the date. Don't wait for the movie/play/gator-wrestling to end. Take her. It would be rude not to.

If it's not going well, you have to either a) turn it around fast or b) cut your losses.

Here are some signs to watch for that it's going poorly: Is she giving you blank stares, like you're speaking in some kind of moon-man language? Is she starting to tell you things like she has to get up early or she's really tired? Or is she constantly answering her cell phone? Then, my friend, it's not going well.

To turn it around, you have to reach deep in the playbook. Avoid any instant replay of the date and go right for the big issues. "Look, maybe it's me, maybe it's you, I don't know, but I saw something in you the other night, something special, that made me ask you out. And that thing isn't here. We can call it a wash and go home, or we can get a couple drinks in us and talk about what went wrong, because the girl I met the other night is worth keeping around."

And you'd better mean it. I'm telling you, you say this to a woman, she is either going to fall madly in love with you or become really, really uncomfortable. By that I mean she may start throwing things. Either way, there's no going back to small talk.

To cut your losses, tell her about a guy you know who would be perfect for her. This guy does not have to actually exist. Promise to call her to set it up; never call.

CLOSING THE DEAL

Thanks to me, you are about to get lucky. You have found the girl who is right for you, and you are at the threshold. You're literally standing at her threshold—the door to her house—but I was being metaphorical. The threshold is . . .

THE FIRST KISS

To a man, the first kiss is the moment you begin to crack open the female safe. But to a woman, the first kiss is the moment she will return to in her mind whenever you piss her off and she has to calm herself and remember how tender you can be. The better you make it, the more of your shit she will be willing to put up with. On the flip side, you kinda have to live up to it. If you execute a John-Wayne-in-*The-Quiet-Man* kiss, you can't turn into a lump on the couch next week.

Make eye contact. Decide which side your nose will go on, look at the lips, then lean in slowly and kiss her. If her tongue goes in your mouth first, you win (see, anything can be competitive, if you're a guy!).

KISS HER UNTIL YOU'RE DONE

Don't let her pull away from the kiss first. If she pulls back, you say as charmingly as you can with a twinkle in your eye: "I'll let you know when I'm done." It's confident and strong, and she may like that but don't stay there forever. (If she doesn't get pissed, you can use it later. "Of course I'm selfish! You knew I was selfish the first time we kissed!")

So you've finished kissing her. Now you have to say something.

GOOD	BAD
"We're not going to do anything you don't want to do."	"You had the fish, didn't you?"

"I want to be with you. Right now."	"Can you kiss like that from your knees?"
"I've been imagining that ever since I met you."	"I don't care if you have crabs, let's do it."
"Damn, girl!"	"I was in *K-9*."

THE DRIVE HOME

This is the most important part of the date. If it was a bad date, it's time for you to beat off into the steering wheel to a Sheryl Crow song. Damn, she sings sexy. Remember to stay off the highways. Drive on surface streets without too much lighting.

If it went well, this is your time to think about the girl you just spent the evening with. Do you want a second date? A third? You'll know this if after the third date you haven't pulled out your Sheryl Crow CD. The girl may even have it at her house.

I said earlier to make sure you planned to take her out on a weeknight. The reason is not only does she have to *earn* Saturday night, but you want her wondering who you are with and what you are doing on Saturday night. Saturday night is for you and your buddies to get drunk, act stupid and laugh at your friends who beat off to Sheryl Crow CDs. If you're out on a Saturday night and find yourself wishing you were out with the chick instead of your buddies, guess what? You've been bit by the love bug. You've got a Saturday night gal.

Truthfully, you probably had a sense that she was "that" girl right from the start. You probably didn't even sleep with her right away. You wanted to "get to know her as a person," right? Bull. She was getting to know *you*. It's like those labor unions that accept you under a trial membership, but don't give you your union card for thirty days so that they can check out your employment history, credit report and stuff like that. Seriously, dude, she's going to Google your ass, so don't give her your middle name unless you want your arrest record to pop up.

But what is it about a woman that separates a "date" from a "girlfriend"? That's a question you need to keep asking yourself after every date. Because every guy is looking for something different.

It's hard to say what I was looking for exactly. I know I had a real good idea of what I was looking to *not* find in a woman. I didn't want someone who was going to compete with me, be uncooperative, disrespect me in public, get in the way of my work and try to change me *too* much (all women try to change men, but it's a matter of degrees). Basically, I wanted someone who would keep the bitching and nagging to a minimum. I suppose what I was really looking for was kindness. I was looking for someone to accept me for who I am, someone who has a good sense of humor and someone who believes in family.

Stevie B. heard that list and said, "You've got too many

rules. You know what I'm looking for? Someone with big tits who won't steal my stuff." Everyone has their own list, but the fact remains, you're going to know when you find that woman.

On the upside, there are some things you can do with your gal that you can't do with your buddies. Which brings us to the next chapter.

!WARNING!

The following chapter contains explicit, albeit hilarious material. It may be unsuitable to young people or people who are just uptight. I'm not saying there's anything wrong with being uptight, I'm just saying if you are one of those people, own up to it and skip ahead to the next chapter. I am serious. You know who you are. I am talking to you. But just to be safe, I'm talking about the following people specifically:

If you are under the age of eighteen, you should not read this chapter.

If you are over the age of sixty, you should not read this chapter.

If you have been to church in the past six months, you should not read this chapter.

Orthodox Bishop Ilya of Philomelion, who baptized me, should not read this chapter.

Marge Hart in Elk Grove, Illinois and any of the seniors who are regulars at the senior center should not read this chapter.

John Beck's grandmother should not read this chapter. In fact, no one's grandmother should read this chapter.

If you are the governor of California weighing a bid for the presidency with me as your running mate, you're going to love it, but keep it away from Maria.

Any executive at Touchstone Television or the American Broadcasting Company, or anyone working in Hollywood, who may at some point in the future consider casting me in a family-oriented project, should not read this chapter.

If you are a party to any lawsuit involving me, you should not read this chapter.

The entire state of Kansas should not read this chapter.

If you are one of my wife's friends, you should not read this chapter.

If you are my wife, you should not read this chapter.

If you are my daughter, reading this book fifteen years in the future because it is now required reading at most major universities, *do not read this chapter.* Give it to your brother.

Finally, if you are that really hot chick from *Lost,* read this chapter. Then call me.

CHAPTER TEN

SEX AND THE SINGLE MAN OVER EIGHTEEN

Early in the morning at the break of day
You and me can wail away
Ooooh baby, ohhh baby
It ain't hot weather that makes me stick to you

—"Hot Weather Blues," Robert Dade/William Ford/
W. Thurman

When you're an A-list Hollywood movie star rumored to have a huge penis, you start to collect a long history of sexual conquests. (Even if you did pay a publicist to plant the huge penis rumor. Okay, maybe you even paid the publicist to create stories of sexual conquest, but let's not let facts cloud our judgment. The important thing to remember is that there is a little phrase known as "star fuckers," and I don't think I've ever heard the expression "average Joe fuckers." I rest my case.)

Several years ago, I was having steamy sex about ten times a day with a beautiful model in Miami's South Beach.

Unfortunately, it was simulated sex, and she was the body double for the lead actress in a movie I was filming. When we weren't grinding, we would sit around the lunch table talking about sex as though we were discussing how to hit a better second serve. During these lunches, the model and I discovered we had something in common: We both loved to sleep with women. One day the subject of oral sex came up, and she talked about how good lesbians were at oral sex. They have the unique perspective of being a woman and having a woman. So I asked her what her secret was and she shared it with me.

Try this at home. Take your index finger and rub it against the tip of your tongue. Feel how coarse and rough that is? Now take the same finger and rub it against the bottom of your tongue. Soft and smooth, right? The clitoris has like a thousand times more nerve endings than a fingertip. It's God's way of making it up to women for not being able to pee in the woods and having to put up with getting a period every month. Think what a difference the bottom of the tongue would make on the clitoris!

The bottom-of-the-tongue thing takes a while to train yourself to do, but once you master it . . . you will have a very, very grateful partner. And there is nothing better than a grateful naked woman. But be warned: Once you execute the back-of-the-tongue maneuver, there is no going back. She'll expect it each time, and unfortunately, you will always be thinking of me.

So if you want to learn how to be great in the sack,

befriend a lesbian. I find that most guys don't really care about technique. What they want to know about is the really important stuff, like how to get a woman to consent to sex in the first place.

If a ram wants to get laid, all he has to do is knock every other male in the herd with his horns. We humans must endure a much more complicated ritual to get our rocks off. It's called foreplay.

Let me be clear: Foreplay is not the thirty seconds you spend playing with a girl's nipples before you mount her. That foreplay is a feminist invention created to further promote the idea that we're supposed to be pleasuring *them*.

Foreplay is everything you say or do to a woman *before* you have sex with her. This can range anywhere from a twenty-minute conversation in a bar to six months of dating followed by a quickie marriage in Vegas.

But where does foreplay end and sex begin? Every man has a girl he thinks he could've bedded, but didn't. Maybe she said something suggestive or touched your arm a certain way and you weren't sure what it meant, so you didn't follow up and nothing happened. It's called a yellow light.

Most women we deal with have the red light on. If men really ran the world, we'd all be humping 24/7. Chicks put the red light on to keep us from banging them all day long—and to maintain some order in the world. Did you ever notice that even if you are living with a woman, she always puts on a robe or wraps up in a towel after stepping out of the shower? That's because she knows that if she walks around naked, you will jump her.

The green light is the moment you know, without a shadow of a doubt, that you're going to have sex with a girl.

Despite all the advances of the sexual revolution, green lights are still extremely rare unless you're willing to pay cash. More often than not what we get is a yellow light, which lets you know that a woman would like to have sex while being vague enough that you have to pursue the matter to confirm her interest. If you miss the sign, she doesn't feel she's been rejected. It's just a miscommunication.

The problem is that a yellow light can mean three things: 1) I want to fuck you, 2) I want to fuck with your head, 3) I am barely aware you're alive and would be repulsed to know that you're thinking I might want to fuck you. As with traffic lights, it's always tough to gauge a yellow light. If you speed up, that red light could snap on and you'll spend eight goddamned hours in traffic school listening to some putz explain to you how to merge onto the freeway.

Figuring out the signals gets so confusing and frustrating that many guys blow it and melt down before the green light finally appears.

Has it ever been as simple as a woman coming up to you and saying "Would you like to have sex with me?" No. Even if that did happen, you wouldn't go for it. You'd figure something was up and if you went home with her, you'd wake up in a bathtub with your kidneys in a cooler on a plane to Indonesia.

More importantly, chicks can't do that (Not the kidney thing. That absolutely happens. I'm talking about the "I want to do you" approach). If they did, they'd have to live with the shame of thinking they are a slut. And, yes, in chick logic, being a slut is a bad thing. If they aren't easy, they have power and dignity. (Dignity . . . I hate that word! It always gets in the way.) You used to have to *marry* a girl to bang her. We've made strides, guys, but I'm here to tell you, women are still holding us down.

The point is that our consciousness revolves around getting some stank on the hang low. We exercise to attract mates. We go to work to make money to attract mates. What made you buy the car you're driving? How do you choose your watering holes? Hell, why do guys follow their passions? Do you think Van Gogh really needed thirty-seven canvases of sunflowers for his apartment? No! He knew it made chicks wet to watch him paint. Christ, he cut off his ear and sent it to a chick.

We're obsessed with sex, and it starts at a young age. Even little boys play with their dicks. I have two sons, and I wish it wasn't true, but believe me, it is. They start when they are about two, between diaper changes. You know when men stop playing with their dicks? Me neither. I haven't found one who's stopped yet—and I know some old dudes.

Chicks aren't obsessed with sex, and they aren't wired to have dirty sex. They're wired to make love. They are wired for relationships, and when you are in a relationship you are making love. When she's not in a relationship and is just doing some guy, she feels like a slut.

Now I know that making love and fucking sound like the same thing, but they aren't. And getting laid is different from fucking.

Getting laid is when you bring a new chick to bed with you. Fucking is what you do with girls that you've already laid. Making love is what you do with your wife while you're thinking about CNN's Heidi Collins.

Which reminds me of my next point: women faking their orgasms. This is how we can even the playing field between men and women.

Many a bitter breakup has climaxed (for lack of a better word) with the woman shouting "I faked all my orgasms" in a crowded restaurant. Maybe not many, but at least one. In 1993. At Le Dome on Sunset in LA . . . that's a story for another day.

My point is that this "insult" has become the ultimate slight to a man's potency. It can send lesser men into a downward spiral of self-doubt, lack of confidence and compulsive masturbation. Come on, at least one of you is a compulsive masturbator. Just me? Okay, okay, let's just move on.

The fact that a chick faking her orgasms is considered a man's fault is just further proof that sexual politics are heavily balanced in favor of the girls. I mean, you're both naked. You're both aroused. You're both *trying* to orgasm. If she doesn't get there, how can that be your fault? Still, it remains the nuclear bomb of breakup technology. But, guys, you have weapons, too.

Let's say you're having sex with a girl. Your mind starts to wander. Suddenly an image of Rachel, the girl from your office with the nice ass, on her knees in front of the copier trying to clear a paper jam pops into your head—her firm ass shaking back and forth as she wrestles the stray sheet from the feeder. Before you know it, you've blown your load. Because you were in your girlfriend? No! Because you were in the copy room, bending Rachel over the fax machine while CNN's Heidi Collins stroked your balls.

Then your girlfriend smirks at you before you fall dead asleep, as if to say, "See how good I make you feel." But how in the hell does she get credit for that? If she had left the bed and stuck a dirty sock over your dick, you would have come just as hard. The only thing she really contributed was friction.

So if you really are feeling a loss of power and want to change the power dynamic in bed, try this: Have sex with your girlfriend and don't come. That's right: *Don't come.*

Think about this. Men come every time, and women take it for granted. Women have an ego when it comes to sex. Think how much power you feel when a woman comes. It's the same for her. Watch how she flips out if you don't finish. Tell her, "It's okay, baby, I don't need to come every time." You'll be lying, but from then on she will make sure you pop.

Here's the problem with this power play. You've got to be able not to come. How do you *not* come? Gentlemen, it's a real discipline. I've had the strength to abstain a couple times. You are not going to be able to do this all the time. To do it more than once, you may need to consult an expert, and no one is better at not spewing their junk than male porn stars.

Is there a more tense work environment than having to get wood in front of thirty grips and electricians in order to start your workday? What makes a guy a true porn star is managing to not trigger until the crew is ready for the money shot. Being a Hollywood player of sorts, I sometimes move in these circles, so I asked a porn star how he holds out. He told me about the Glurk.

The Glurk is the feeling that comes right before you come. It's like the rumble you hear right before Old Faithful erupts. When the porn star feels the Glurk, he pictures putting his teeth on the curb of a freeway or something equally disturbing. This throws everything in reverse. Your dick will be so confused you might not come for a week.

Challenge your Glurk and then tell your girlfriend you've finished without finishing. After that she'll *wonder* if she can make you come, then *hope* you're about to come, then *need* to rock your world.

My point is that men need to shake things up. I mean, we're already responsible for seeking out partners. Then we're supposed to make sure they get what they need? What kind of a setup is that? That's like going to the grocery store and then being told by a steak that it doesn't like the way you chew it.

Don't think all of this is anti-woman. I think sex is much better with a girl. I just think men have let themselves get fooled into thinking they are having sex for the woman's sake. Women do not suffer this illusion, so why should men?

To illustrate, I will draw from Stevie B.'s formative years. Stevie B. once had a chick as a roommate. She was a beautiful cocktail waitress who came into his life innocently enough—by answering his ad for a roommate to share an apartment. The arrangement was strictly about splitting rent, but after a couple weeks the girl came to his room wearing a teddy and told him point-blank: "We are going to do it sooner or later, so we might as well do it now." Stevie B.'s response: "Great. Let me just finish up with Pam here, and I'll be right with you."

So, for the next two weeks, they went at it like bunnies. Every time, this chick would scream and moan and cry out so loud that he would cover her mouth, fearing that the neighbors would call the police. This screaming and moaning fed his ego. Stevie B. felt like a sex god. He walked down the street on his toes because he was certain he was the best lover in the world. Girls he passed would shoot him looks because a woman can sense when a guy is getting it good, and they're intrigued.

After two weeks, Stevie B. and the cocktail waitress both decided to stop doing it. Everything was cool, and they went back to being roommates. Eventually, she brought a guy home to her room. Stevie B. was cool with that because, after all, the thing he had with her was just a fling. Besides, he knew she would never get it as good with another guy as she got it from him. But just as he was basking in his glory, he heard the *same* screaming, the *same* moaning, the *same* crying out. The girl was making the exact same noises for the new guy!

Stevie B. realized he didn't have a magic cock. He wasn't a sex god. He realized "that's just the way she fucks." We all can learn from Stevie B. When you are making mad love to a woman and she is going crazy, never lose perspective. Don't believe your own bullshit. Don't believe your own unjustly inflated ego. It's dangerous. I know; I've done it. When women made me feel that I was great in the sack, I married them!

You guys have been doing such a good job of reading these long informative passages that I'm going to give you something to clip and save now. [Simone: No need to spell-check this part, it's mostly curse words—JB]. Here's the real man's sex glossary, which is provided for prurient interests only.

JIM'S SEX GLOSSARY

Mutual Satisfaction—Giving the impression to your partner that you intend to help her orgasm.

Prep Work—Physical contact with the rest of a woman's

body required to enhance your contact with her vagina. Often referred to by women as "foreplay." Involves:

Firing a shot across the bow—During the pre-sex makeout, moving your hands slowly but steadily over her crotch with clothes on to establish a foothold in the region.

Saying hello to the girls—Using your tongue to stimulate her nipples. And if you want to drive a chick crazy, just work on one.

The Yellow Pages—As in letting your fingers do the walking—though in this case it's more of a thrust and swirl than a walk.

The Work Day—The time you spend naked with a woman engaging in sexual behavior. This can include lying in bed talking if you're just using it to cover your refractory period. Remember that if you put in more than three hours, you're eligible for a coffee break.

A Shift—Based on the hockey term for the amount of time a player spends on the ice playing the game. A shift, in this sense, is the amount of time you spend with your penis inside a woman, actually having sex. Note that in the NHL, an average shift is about a minute and a half.

The Pound of Flesh—This means the amount of time spent with a woman after sex, where all she really wants is your flesh pressing against her. You essentially become a teddy bear. A POF can range from waiting for her to fall asleep and then slipping out so fast that you forget your shoes, to getting married and having four kids with her.

Those are basic talking points for your typical encounters. But who wants typical? At the zeniths of our bachelorhood, Stevie B. and I turned getting laid into a competitive event. It's sort of like Yahtzee. There are categories to complete, and when you do, you receive a score. It might seem like some of these should count for negative points, but really it's all about playing the game. We kept adding categories until I got married. Technically, I lost, but it was a very, very good game.

The Hat Trick—Based on the hockey term for scoring three goals in one game. A hat trick is pulling off the scheduling feat of having sex with three different women in one twenty-four-hour period. Example: Stevie B. takes Cara out on Friday night. They have sex from 1:00 a.m. until 6:30 (there's a reason I look up to this guy). He meets up with Adriana for Saturday lunch and a nooner. That night, he goes out with Cecilia. If he gets her to bed before 1:00 a.m., he'll have completed the hat trick.

Zen—Anything more than a hat trick in one twenty-four-hour period.

Turkey—Derived from a bowling term for rolling three strikes in a row, it means reaching orgasm with the same girl three times in one Work Day. Note that you cannot achieve a Turkey by yourself. That's called a "Chicken" (see also: "Choking the . . ."). If you get a woman to come three times in one Work Day, it's called "Trying too hard."

Nothing But Net—You meet a girl in a bar, go back to her place to have sex with her, and never see her again.

Yes! And the Foul!—The elusive situation where you bring a girl home and she asks if she can call her girlfriend and invite her over. This should not be confused with "The Marv Albert," which involves wigs and biting.

The Seventh Grade Dance—Having a Work Day with a girl where you're both naked, making out and petting, but she stops it before anyone comes. The name derives from the age when this stops being interesting to a man.

The Pro-Bowl 69—This one starts, as all good sexual activities do, with you lying on your back. However, in this tricky little maneuver, the woman's back is arched, with her stomach pointing to the ceiling. It's a Yogic way to complete the Holy Mouth-Genital-Mouth-Genital Circle.

The Clinton—Achieving orgasm with a woman in a way that allows you to say with a straight face, "I did not have sex with that woman." Typically, this means a blow job or being jerked off, but Stevie B. has found at least seven other methods.

The Graduate—Having sex with a woman at least fifteen years older than you. This may soon be renamed "The Ashton Kutcher."

Bigfoot Sighting—Meeting a woman at least fifteen years older than you that you would actually consider having sex with.

The Woody Allen—Having sex with someone that you're legally allowed to, but probably shouldn't: i.e., a stepsister, your brother's ex-wife, Stevie B.'s mom . . .

The *Washington Post* —She's so hot, and so good in the sack, you have to read the *Washington Post* to keep from finishing early. I have a variation on this called "The *Chicago Tribune*." If I'm looking at a picture of Irv Kupcinet, I'm not going to finish. I don't care what's happening.

Office Goggles —The first day you showed up at your job you surveyed the workplace for hot chicks, but didn't see any. Then one day, you notice that Laura from accounting has a really nice ass. Maybe she's been working out? No, your office goggles are on. Spend enough hours staring at the chicks you work with, and they'll start getting hot. Of course, you're programmed to procreate, so your penis recalibrates its standard for "hot." Here's an important fact to always remember: Your penis does not have eyes. You have to see for it.

The C.S.I. —Waking up with a woman you don't remember meeting the night before and having to piece together what happened. The first thing to do is check for a ring.

Chair Work —Basically, it's you, a willing young lass and a chair. I know what you're saying, everyone's fucked in a chair, right? Well, anyone who's made it this far into this glossary, anyway. Here's the thing, though. The "work" in chair work does not apply to the girl. No, you have to "work" the chair. There are seven distinct positions to have sex in a chair. When you have figured them all out, you take a seat and tell the girl there are four more for her to find. Only then will you have worked the chair. I highly advise you to only do chair work in a hotel. Unless, of course, you have some really good Scotchgarding at home.

The U.N.—The U.N. is not a sexual feat as much as a life-long goal. The idea is to have sex with a black chick, a Latina, an Asian, a Jew, an Arab and an Eskimo.

The Rainbow Connection—As the U.N., this is a long-term goal. The idea is to have sex with a brunette, a blonde and a redhead, but the color of the hair on their head is ir-relevant. I thought for sure I had completed the Rainbow Connection when I brought home a redhead, only to find out that she had completely waxed down there. That prick Stevie B. refused to give me credit.

Bunny Boiler—Sleeping with a chick you know for a fact is insane.

Corner Store—A woman whom you can call upon any hour of the day or night, make a quick stop and leave.

The Black Hole—A woman you cannot stop having sex with. Each time you see her, you tell her and yourself that this is the last time, but then you wind up on her stoop at 2:00 a.m. the next week.

The Bridge on the River Kwai—Remember how in that movie Alec Guinness spends like five years building a bridge for the Japanese, only to have Bill Holden blow it up in the last scene? It's ironic because they're both supposed to be fighting for the Allies.

Here's how our "Bridge" works. You're at a bar and you watch your buddy work a girl all night. Finally, she agrees to go home with him. He excuses himself to take a piss and while he's gone, you leave with the chick.

The Abu Ghraib—Doing a chick from behind and, without her knowing, snapping a picture with your camera phone of you, in her, giving the thumbs up sign. An extra point if you're smoking a cigarette.

The Bi-Polar—Having sex with a chick who has said she hates you and hopes you die within the last twenty-four hours. You cannot propose just to get her to sleep with you. Paul was pissed when he found out about that technicality.

The Roberto Duran—Having sex with a chick for so long and so hard that she finally says *"no mas."*

The Jimmy "Superfly" Snuka—Named after the famed professional wrestler. This is where you run in from the bathroom, take off from the foot of the bed and attempt to land not only *on* your partner, but *in* your partner. This is not something you want to attempt with Lara Flynn Boyle. She needs some meat on her bones. Several comrades have sustained serious injury attempting the Superfly. Only Stevie B. has stuck the landing.

But that's all just gross bullshit that guys tell other guys in sports bars. Truth is, none of that is going get you laid or help you find a mate. To do that, you're going to have to learn to talk to women. Respect women. And listen to them. You are going to have to know a lot more than which side of your tongue to use. First of all, you are going to have to ask a woman out on a date. So get to it. You may strike out a couple times, but relax. After all, they weren't going to sleep with you anyway. They're all lesbians, remember?

BOOK THREE

THE BOOK OF LOVE, ACCORDING TO JIM

CHAPTER ELEVEN

ARE YOU READY FOR A LONG-TERM RELATIONSHIP? TAKE THIS SIMPLE QUIZ

Gotta have an angel of your own
To be there for you when things go wrong
To make you feel special
Love ya strong
An angel of your own

—"Angel," Glen Clark

If you've watched my TV show—and, let's face it, there's no way someone thought to buy you this book unless you are glued to the TV when my giant head shows up Tuesday nights—you know I love a good junior high–level joke. One of my favorites involves a schoolteacher, a kindergarten class and a kid named Dirty-Mouthed Johnny.

The class was learning about the alphabet. As she went from A to Z the teacher was asking students to use a word that started with that letter. She'd ask if anyone knew a word that started with "A," and when Johnny's hand went up, she knew he was gonna say "asshole." Then the B-word, "bitch." Then the C-word, "cocksucker." And so on. When the teacher finally got to "R" and saw Johnny raising his hand. She couldn't think of any curse words that started with R, so she called on him. He replied, "Rat . . . with a big-ass dick!"

Well, guess what, men. There's another R-word we all know. "Relationship." And more often than not, it's harder for us to say than any curse word in any language.

Relationship.

And you know why it's hard to say? Because men love chasing chicks. Love "gettin' down on it." Love smelling our own farts. But hate, hate, hate relationships. Besides getting our stones busted by our buddies who can't find a chick, we don't know how to handle relationships. And more importantly, we don't know how to handle ourselves once we are in them.

Do you think you're ready to make a commitment? To clean out a couple drawers for her stuff? To limit yourself to just one vagina? Should you even be thinking about it? Are you thinking about it anyway?

If you'd taken my advice, you would be done with the book. You wouldn't need to read the last section. But I'm kinda glad you didn't because I really have saved the best for the last. Except for the sex glossary; there's no topping that.

Because you've come this far, you know where we're headed, so let's cut to the chase. Sharpen your pencil one last time for your final quiz.

1. Picture yourself with this woman five years from now. Close your eyes and do it. Were you:
   a) Holding hands on a beach, feeling the deep sense of love that only a true commitment to another person can give you?
   b) Getting yelled at as if you had just shit on the bedspread for doing something you have done all your life without a second thought?
   c) Coming home from work to a clean house, a hot meal, and someone interested in your stories? (This vision would be in black-and-white.)
   d) Nervous and intimidated, yet somehow looking forward to it, like the child of an abusive alcoholic at Christmas?

None of these are wrong. A real grown-up relationship is many things to many people, so I will just give you points however I want. Holding hands on the beach with a deep sense of longing is the vision of a cockeyed optimist—good luck to you. Even more luck to the poor realist who pictures himself being badgered by his woman. The clean house scenario is pure TV fantasy, but if you chose this, you can add a point for believing in TV because that's where I make my money. But I think the correct answer for the point is d): On your toes, but expecting good things.

2. Which of these things will you absolutely have to do once you're in a long-term relationship?
   a) Take an interest in wallpaper design.
   b) Look around before farting.
   c) Buy the Tampax.
   d) Submit.

If you don't look around before farting now, don't start. She knew that about you going in, so she has no leg to stand on. If you don't want to buy the Tampax, I think you're making a big deal out of nothing, but that's your big deal, and you've earned it. And you never submit! You cooperate, sure. You acquiesce on occasion. In emergencies, you may even withdraw completely. But never submit! Surprisingly, the correct answer is a) because taking an interest in wallpaper design is part of making decisions as a couple about things that only one of you cares about. Even if you don't care, each of you will still have to go through the motions of considering the options to allow her to arrive at a decision. You will do it about wallpaper; she will do it about leaf blowers, or computers, or garage door openers. That's just how it works.

3. Which of these things will you never do once you're serious?
   a) Keira Knightley.

b) Put your feet on anything but the floor—well, that and a stepladder when she needs something fixed.

c) Make a decision without thinking, "Would she be cool with this?"

d) Watch DVDs and masturbate with glorious abandon.

While it's true you will never do Keira Knightley, it's not because you're in a relationship. It's because she can choose any guy on the planet and you learned how to be a man by reading a book by an actor. The correct answer is c) because every decision that you make affects her, directly or indirectly. A lot of times, you will say "I don't care if she's cool with it or not! I deserve to put my feet up and watch a Keira Knightley DVD," but at least you thought of her. That's the important thing—considering her. Just a simple act of consideration can sometimes mean everything to a girl and most of the time it's all they need.

4. Who are your relationship role models?
   a) My what?!
   b) Henry VIII.
   c) The handsome, lovable scamp from *According to Jim.*
   d) Jerry down the street with the great lawn.

It's c). What, did you forget who's writing the book? TV's Jim fucks up a lot, but he loves his wife, he takes care of his kids, and you know he and his wife are happier together than they would be apart. But I suppose a) is okay too, so I can't in good conscience deprive you of a point for that answer. On the list of things to envy about a guy, his relationship comes in pretty low. If you said Henry VIII, take away one point for being a wise-ass, but add it back for knowing some English History. (I had Simone Google "shitty husband" to find him.) As for Jerry down the street, if his relationship is so great, then why is he always out front with the hose?

    5. A healthy relationship means:
       a) Neither of you get colds anymore.
       b) You set aside time to meet her emotional needs.
       c) Lots of sex and no yelling.
       d) Doing what she says until I scream at her to leave me alone.

All of these indicate a healthy relationship. Even if you are a complete pussy and answered d), give yourself a point.

    6. You've been together three years, and it has been pretty hard work, but you two are in a good place. When can you start coasting?
       a) Now.
       b) Never.
       c) I've been coasting the whole time. I just said that

"pretty hard work" thing because you always hear that "relationships are hard work!"

d) Is this a trick question?

Yes, it is a trick question, but b) is obviously the right answer. Even if, hypothetically, you were to coast, you would never, ever admit that. It would be like waving a red flag at a bull. A bull you are sleeping with.

7. What if you take this all the way? How will your wife be different from your girlfriend, provided she is the same woman?

a) Same chick, bigger ass.

b) You know how if you rent a house, you don't give a shit about anything, but when you own your house, every little problem with it makes you nuts? You're the house.

c) You know how you ride a Jet Ski on vacation, and you think, "This would be great to have all the time!"? So you buy one but it just sits there, and you feel like you wasted your money because it wasn't as fun as you thought it would be, then it gets old, and newer, sexier models come out that you think would be so much better and your friends would be envious of? She's the Jet Ski.

d) You know how when you were a kid, you loved candy, and all you wanted all the time was that sweet, sweet candy? Then you got older and you started to appreciate potatoes, in all their many forms, and steak, and even the occasional salad, just to mix it up? Your girlfriend is candy. Your wife is Thanksgiving dinner.

This is tricky because all of these are technically accurate. This question is a matter of perspective. How you look at things has a lot to do with how she acts. If you're talking to a single guy, you'd probably say same chick, bigger ass because it's funny, quick and makes you seem worldly and wise. But the size of her ass is not your main problem. Sure, bring it up to her, every day if necessary, but make sure she knows that you're "joking." The answer for the point is d) and you are a (probably portly) man after my own heart. You like having a girlfriend for the fun things you do together. When you find someone you like doing the shitty things with, that's your wife.

8. Before you get too cocky, she sees you differently too. How?
   a) The way you dress is a reflection on her. So you're not wearing *that,* are you?
   b) There's no such thing as a "casual remark." Your every utterance will be scrutinized like Alan Greenspan's.
   c) You still aren't a cat person. But her cat really is different. It is. It really is!
   d) All of the above.

The answer is e) **+**. The plus is for the new things you will find out about every day. You won't feel different, you won't look different, you won't even be different, but you're not looking through her eyes. To do that, you would have to get inside her head, and that's not someplace you want to go. Ever.

9. Sex in a committed, long-term relationship is:
    a) the only thing between her and the sidewalk.
    b) a faraway dream I hope one day to achieve.
    c) not that important.
    d) great, until your girlfriend finds out.

It sounds harsh, but a) is the answer. You don't want a roommate, a "best friend," a business partner in the home, or a buddy. You want a lover, and so does she. People will tell you "sex doesn't solve any problems." Maybe not, but it sure makes you feel good so you can deal with whatever the problem is. You may hear some barbershop philosopher say of a woman, "Nothing wrong with her a good fuck wouldn't cure." That old man is right. I don't know why he hangs around the barbershop as much as he does, but he's right.

10. The single most important thing about relationships is:
    a) I don't know, listening or something.
    b) sex.

c) winning.

d) compassion.

It's b) and if you got it wrong, pay attention, dammit! I just spent all of question nine getting you to have sex, and then you go and answer something other than sex. It's sex! You may be thinking, "But what about mutual respect, what about companionship, what about love?" Here's my answer: Love without sex is friendship, sex without love is spring break, and if you want companionship, get a dog. You will avoid many of life's pitfalls if you just have regular sex with your beloved. They just won't come up. If they do come up, you will have the trust to work your way through them. How do you know that? Because you have had your mouths on each other's genitals, *and* you have decided which cable package to subscribe to. The person you do these two hugely different—but very important—things with is the person you need in your life.

Now for the scoring. Honestly, if you answered the last two questions correctly and you are having consistent, mutually satisfying sex with your girlfriend (and *only* your girlfriend), you can skip the last section. But the book's paid for and there's no "I'm having sex with my girlfriend" rebate, so why not keep reading? You might learn something. If you missed the last two, go make crazy love to your lady, then come back and read the last section.

CHAPTER TWELVE

IF YOU DON'T LEAVE ME ALONE, I'M GONNA FIND SOMEBODY THAT WILL

If you don't leave me alone,
I'm gonna find somebody that will
What you do with your business
Until it starts giving me chills
If you don't leave me alone
I'm gonna find somebody that will

—"If You Don't Leave Me Alone, I'm
Gonna Find Somebody That Will,"
Delbert McClinton and Sony Fortner

Because I had mastered all the techniques I explained for you in Book Two, I was dating several women when I met my future wife and mother to two of my children and the most beautiful woman in the world, Jenny.

We dated, but eventually I wasn't scheduling Jenny for Wednesday night dates anymore. She had earned Saturday.

I realized that I liked being around her more than all the other women and even more than my buddies. I revealed to her that she had ascended the ranks to number one. I thought she might be touched, moved to tears even. Instead she just snapped, "So who's number two?"

A couple months after seizing the top ranking, her birthday came up. I told her I would "take her out or something." The day before her birthday, Eddy, my agent, called. I put him on speaker with Jenny in the room. He told me that he had arranged an important meeting for me and that it was scheduled for dinner the following night. I explained that was a bad time, because it was Jenny's birthday.

Eddy growled into the phone, "It took me four months to set this meeting up. It's the only day he's in town. Buy her a big fucking gift and she'll forget all about it."

"I don't think she's going for that," I explained. "Why don't you tell her?"

"Am I on the box? *Am I on the goddamn speakerbox?!*"

"Yes, Eddy, you are," I confessed.

His tone shifted, "Hi, Jenny, how are you? Happy birthday. What a big day, huh?"

By the time he got off the phone, Jenny had agreed that I could go meet this guy I was supposed to meet *after* I took her out. Eddy kept me working after *Wild Palms;* he can sell anything.

I got off the phone with Eddy. Jenny was verging on

tears. I told her it was a really important meeting. Finally, she sadly left the house. I chased her to her car and talked her back into the house.

"Hold on, hold on. I guess you need someone to take you out the night before your birthday too, huh? I didn't know it was such a big deal. I mean, of course I want to see you on your birth*day*. I just didn't realize you celebrated a birth-*week*." I let out a big sigh and said, "Okay. I'll take you out to-night, too. Why aren't all these friends you keep telling me you have calling to take you out for your birthweek?" Of course, that brought her to the brink of tears again.

I told her not to worry, I was going to take her to a place called Musso & Frank's. It's an L.A. landmark, a great restau-rant, and most importantly an easy spot to get a cab, be-cause she would need to take one home so I could go to my meeting.

"Why are you doing this?" she stammered. I explained it gave me a false feeling of empowerment. She didn't under-stand. Finally, I agreed that it wouldn't be right to make her take a cab home. I would drive her. I told her this was really throwing a monkey wrench in my schedule. I would have to stop at the House of Blues and tell the Hollywood player I was going to meet that I was going to be late because "Jenny doesn't take cabs."

I pulled my car up to the House of Blues and hopped out. I got to the door and stopped. I came back to the car and, half sighing, asked, "Do you want to come in?"

Jenny hurriedly got out of the car. The guy was a notorious playboy. She knew there would be women all over, and she wanted to walk in on my arm to mark her territory.

We walked into the club and, as the doors flew open, a hundred of Jenny's friends, family and loved ones screamed, *"Surprise!"*

In an instant she realized it had all been a ruse. The call from Eddy. My supposed meeting. My cold treatment. The cab ride. All an elaborate con built especially for her by me. She turned to me, the hero who had given her the fantasy, and said, "I cannot believe you let me wear *this!*"

Jenny glowed all evening. The party was a hit. Then something funny happened. I was at the bar watching her enjoy all her friends when her father caught my eye. He looked right at me and gave me a slight nod, as if to say, "Thanks for being so good to my baby." I know it might seem like I should have realized it when I spent six months and several grand planning the party for her, but it wasn't until I saw the nod from her dad that it hit me. I realized I was the "boyfriend" now.

"Oh shit," I thought, "I'm in a relationship." This girl was the one. She wasn't just the best one I was dating. She was the one I was in love with. It was time to get serious. Stevie B. had warned me this day would come, but I still wasn't ready. I only knew one thing: I didn't want to fuck it up. I had made a deal with myself that I would never get divorced again. To keep that promise, I would have to make sure I built a good foundation for this relationship.

Now, if you've gotten through Books One and Two, you're going to eventually find yourself in this spot. You'll suddenly realize you're the boyfriend. You've got yourself a good chick. A Saturday night gal. You don't want things to get screwed up. But if you don't watch yourself, it will.

Before I get into the modern relationship, I think it's important to give you a historical background on how relationships got started. Mostly because I like writing about cavemen.

Back in the days before ESPN, Early Man started a relationship by walking out of his cave, finding the cave chick with the biggest set of cave boobs, fighting off all his buddies for her, whacking her over the head with some blunt object and dragging her back to his cave.

Victory!

At least Early Man thought so. I mean, now he wouldn't have to go down to the stream and wait for some chick to show up with laundry. But he soon found out that once you dragged a woman back to your cave, things got a lot more complicated than when you just humped them in the stream. Because a relationship is different than dating.

After getting his cave chick, Early Man would provide for his lady by venturing out of the caves and braving opposing tribes, dinosaurs, plagues, swarms of locusts, snakes, storms, and man-eating flying squirrels in order to bring meat back to the cave. When he arrived home from this grueling trek, during which he risked life and limb, he was greeted by the sight of his woman standing at the mouth of the cave with her hands on her hips, shaking her head and muttering, "You forgot to pick up the firewood, didn't you?"

When every second outside the cave meant you were at risk of a man-eating flying squirrel carrying you back to his cave, you learned to prioritize. Cavemen would only go out when absolutely necessary, and then gather only that which was absolutely necessary. And even in modern times, to the irritation of their wives, men didn't carry shopping lists. This is an evolutionary holdover from the time when if you couldn't remember to pick something up while you're out, the item wasn't important enough to bring back. Also, no caveman ever had to buy tampons.

Meanwhile, women would sit in the caves, drawing on the walls and thinking of all the things it would be nice to have. Sure she enjoyed the wooly mammoth meat, but wouldn't it be nice to have a fire to cook it over? Once it was cooked, she started thinking it would just be so great to have some delicious vegetables to eat with it. Then she started thinking she could go for something sweet afterward. Eventually, she contemplated how great it would be if her husband had somewhere else to take a dump other than next to their bed . . . you know, once her man invented beds. Soon, the whole family would have a latrine outside and it would occur to her that she really should have something to cover her feet when she's out there. And certainly the invention of shoes couldn't have been more than a few days old before the first woman wondered if he couldn't make them just a little bit "cuter."

Over time, these things were added to the list of what was "absolutely necessary." Not because Early Man thought he needed these things. He needed her and believed that if he brought these things back to the cave, the nagging would end after his next hunt. All men wanted was some peace and quiet. And *SportsCenter*.

Some of you wonder why Early Man put up with it. He was doing all the hunting and fishing. Why not just get rid of the women? Believe me, it was discussed, but the cavemen decided that they needed women too much for cooking, companionship, ego-stroking and sex. Early Man might've been whipped, but they weren't stupid. Sex for meat? Fair enough. You fuck one triceratops, you learn that lesson real quick.

There are many things we can learn from our friend Early Man. First and foremost, at any point in that history lesson did you hear any sappy talk about how a relationship is a "special bringing together of souls when two people become one in a union of the heart?" Of course you didn't. Because that's bullshit written by some Nancy-pants. No, no, my friends. Early Man gave his woman some of his meat because whatever she was doing for him was worth the trade-off.

Okay, before we travel any farther down Relationship Road, you have to ask yourself a hard question: Why are you doing this? Why get into a relationship? And unlike the questions I made you ask yourself before, in this case, there is only one right answer. There are lots of wrong answers, however. For example:

Loneliness—It's okay. Admit it. We've all been there. Even the ol' Belush himself. Over and over again. After my second divorce, I got so bad that Stevie B. and the rest of my guys had to sit me down and give me some rules so I wouldn't just grab the first chick I came across.

They told me I couldn't get into a serious relationship. I had to live alone for a year. I couldn't buy jewelry for any girl that I went out with. And I couldn't allow a woman to sleep over at my place. Tough love? Yes. But it made me self-sufficient. Stevie B. understood that if I couldn't be a man on my own, I couldn't be a man in a relationship. Plus I got to watch the 2:00 a.m. *SportsCenter* with the bed to myself.

Horniness—Every man alive has dated a girl longer than he should have just because she got his rocks off. "A steady piece of ass is not a relationship." Write that down and give it to your best friend. Tell him to throw it back in your face the next time you're dating a hot girl you can't stand to be around.

Sex is almost always good, but sometimes you find a girl who really knows how to ring your bell. Your dick will try to convince you that it means you're meant to be with her. But if right after sex you start wishing she would turn into a six-foot hoagie or your buddies with a stack of poker chips and a deck or cards . . . tell your dick she's got to go. Another piece of ass will be along shortly.

Everyone Else Likes Her—Your mom, your buddies, the

waitress; she has the power to charm everyone. But she's a bitch to you. You assume you're wrong. After all, she keeps reminding you that you're an idiot.

So what's the right reason to be in a relationship? It's really simple. *You dig her.*

This girl has the qualities you are looking for. And you know what these qualities are because you did your homework in Book Two and decided what you wanted in a woman. Early Man picked "big cave boobs" and "the ability to take a whack on the head." Maybe you picked patience, kindness and big boobs. I don't know. You picked 'em, not me. But double-check. Remember, you're an idiot. Your ex-girlfriend told you so.

Okay, so we're straight at this point. You bagged a good chick with the qualities you want in a woman. Now it's all clear sailing, right? Wrong. It's just the beginning. Remember those classes in college where they gave you a list of books to read before you even started taking the class? If you were anything like me, you probably remember feeling like a complete jackass when you walked into class not knowing what the fuck anyone was talking about because you went to Wing Night instead of studying.

That's why you read the first two parts of this book. Now you're on equal footing with your girlfriend. Feels good, doesn't it? It should. But there's still work to be done.

Without Early Man first learning how to handle himself in a relationship, none of us would be here today. You know why? Because some dinosaur would have eaten him and he would never have made cave babies that eventually spawned Man as we know him.

Early Man learned to say, "No." It may have been a grunt. He may have bared his teeth and smacked his cave ass. But his cavewoman knew what he meant.

"No."

Cavewoman's job was to try and get the most out of Early Man to improve their situation. More often than not, her ideas were great. "We need food. Can you kill us some?"

"Yes."

"I need some new clothes for the Slagstones' party. Can you can skin me some?"

"Yes."

"The children are acting up. Can you hit them over the head with a blunt object?"

"Yes."

"I need a new rock to pound the dirt out of our skins. Can you go get one from the river?"

"No. There are several man-eating squirrels out there."

"But I really need a new rock. And there aren't that many squirrels . . ."

"I said no. And what's wrong with the rock you have?"

"It's an outdated model. The Slagstones have a new one."

"No."

"But honey . . ."

"No!" And then our caveman friend bared his teeth and smacked his ass to let his woman know he was unwavering, an early Clint. Oh, sure, she was upset. But she realized her caveman was right when she got the news that Arthur Slagstone had been eaten by a man-eating flying squirrel because his wife sent him out to get decorative berries for the party. And even though she was mad, she respected our caveman's strength for standing his ground. He set boundaries. He established rules for the relationship.

Standing your ground and setting boundaries is how we as men demonstrate strength. And a woman wants a strong man so she feels protected. Our caveman could demonstrate this strength by going out and killing the biggest Wooly Mammoth or warring with local tribes. It's not quite as simple for us modern guys because we can pick up a pizza on the way home and lawyers have made it practically impossible to war with anyone. ("But cavemen did it" does not fly as a defense for getting in a fight with a pedestrian who walked in front of your bike. I found that out the hard way.)

So in order to make sure their men are strong, A. Justin Sterling says, women need to *test us*. And if you want your relationship to work, you have to *pass the test*. It starts with little things: "Wear a sportcoat." "Lift up the toilet seat." "Stop drinking from the milk carton." "Use a coaster for your beer bottle." "Don't fart in public or scratch your balls or swear." In general, she'll start making you more "socially acceptable."

How do you handle these social corrections? Ask yourself: Does it compromise my agreements with myself, my terms? Does what she asks me to do compromise me as a man? Does it compromise me as a man to wear a sportcoat? If the answer is yes, then you need to fight to the death before putting on a sportcoat. But let's face it, most of us could use a few lessons in social graces.

The longer you are in a relationship, however, the tougher the tests become. You don't want to get walked all over, and your girlfriend won't want to be with a guy she can lead around by the nose. You have to set boundaries. Know where your lines have been drawn, and make it clear so people—specifically your new girlfriend—can figure out what flies and what doesn't. Your "Whatever you want, baby" stuff doesn't work anymore.

Boundaries establish limits based on past behavior. I say "past behavior" because someone's gotta do something to you before you know you don't like it. That or someone needs to teach you what your boundaries are. Ideally your parents would do that, but they must not have, otherwise you wouldn't need this book. Don't feel bad. If my parents had done it, I wouldn't be writing it.

Here's an example of how boundaries get established. No one knew "Do not murder me" was a boundary until Cain offed Abel. And it became one helluva boundary. It made it into Moses's Top Ten List, and then into the U.S. Constitution.

So take some time and figure out your boundaries. What crap have you taken that you never want to take again? Here are some suggested boundaries for a long-term relationship that I came up with from my two failed marriages. I call them Belushi's Five Commandments (I was gonna do Ten, but Moses still has the copyright on that and I'm a cheap, cheap man):

Thou Shalt Not Shush. For me, this one's real simple. I hated getting shushed in third grade almost as much as I hate it now. I hate getting shushed when someone is talking on the phone, or when I'm saying something slightly offensive, or when there is a baby in the house, or when someone else wants to speak. If you want your turn to talk, wait for me to finish. Believe me, eventually I'll have to eat something and you can talk all you want. I may even pay attention, depending on how good the sandwich is.

Thou Shalt Not Steal. I draw a big fat hairy line at stealing from me: my money, my stuff, my time, my heart. This goes back to respect. Why would you let someone disrespect you by stealing?

This boundary gets a little fuzzy, however, around dinnertime. I have been known to snag food from any plate within a fork's perimeter of mine. The rule when eating with me is "Keep Your Arms Up and Your Eyes Open." You've been warned.

Thou Shalt Never Banish Me to the Couch. In previous relationships, whenever I got into a fight, you'd find me on the couch. Then I got to thinking, "How come I'm always the one leaving the room to go sleep on the damn couch?" Sure, it's nostalgic to be able to jerk off and fall right asleep, but that's the only upside.

After one routine fight, I said to the girl, "You know what? If you're so damn mad, *you* go sleep on the couch!" I tossed her pillows to her and curled up to go to sleep. She started arguing again. I said in my best Clint voice, "I'm done fighting. Your couch is calling." She was so confused she paced around for a bit, and then crawled into bed. And let me tell you, you've never seen anything as funny as a woman with a big ass doing an angry crawl.

Oh, sure I'd be lying if I said I wasn't worried about getting an ice pick in the back. But I wasn't on that damn couch. Incidentally, whoever said "Never go to bed mad" is full of shit. Angry sleep is still sleep. And why spend all night trying to resolve some crap that will seem silly to both of you in the morning? Watch *The Principal* and look at the bags under my eyes. I was up all night during that film "discussing" and "resolving" with my lady. I would have killed for more than two hours of sleep a night but I had no Clint. I was a pushover. I was a sensitive guy. Luckily I was able to take out my aggressions driving my motorcycle down a school hallway. (It pays to do your own stunts.)

I take it back. I just watched *The Principal* again. I look fabulous.

Thou Shalt Not Compete With Me. Don't compete with me. Chances are, I've been out there competing all day long, so I don't want to have to go back into "battle mode" as soon as I walk in the door. This is a dynamic I will never have in a relationship again. Don't challenge me in a competitive way, because men are all about competition. All we have is competition. Our whole ego is wired around it. We have to win. Every time. If I'm challenged, I'm going to fight to the death. Curly, Clint and Gandhi get thrown out the window and replaced with Conan the Barbarian, whose higher purpose in life was, "to crush my enemies, see them driven before me, and hear the lamentation of their women."

And most importantly: **Thou Shalt Not Expect an Apology for Something I Am Not Sorrieth For.** I think you've heard this one before . . .

Oh, and if you need a breather from defending legitimate boundaries, here's a trick I learned: Lie to make yourself look worse. I was dating this girl and I overheard her say to one of her friends that she hated moustaches. So I started growing one. She bitched and moaned about it for like a week and a half, but I told her I thought it made me look distinguished. She begged and begged me to shave it. I finally "gave in." She felt like she accomplished something, and I didn't have to give up anything I gave that much of a crap about in the first place. She was so happy when I got rid of that big itchy mess that she rewarded me with an entire day of appreciation sex. Clean-shaven. Wink, wink, nudge, boing!

So, you must be thinking, "Wow, Jim. This relationship stuff is great. All I have to do is tell her a bunch of stuff I don't want to do or won't let her do." Think again. There's a whole bunch of stuff you need to do to keep things cool. It's not particularly tough. It's just tough to remember to do them. I'm gonna put them in bold so you can just skim through here in between commercials during football. I'm a helluva guy. What can I say?

Be a Good Listener. Pay attention. Or at least act like you are. And being a good listener is not just about listening. A. Justin Sterling says it's about *how* you listen. Learn to say, "I don't know." Be objective. Stay cool and calm during heated discussions. Don't take things personally. Phrase your thoughts as questions so you don't sound like a demanding jerk: "Wouldn't it work better if we had sex before you put that mud mask on?" And above all else, learn to use what I like to call your "TiVo listening skills." You know how TiVo records whatever show you are watching for a half hour? Do that with your girlfriend. That way you can still watch the game, but when she asks if you are paying attention, you can rewind and parrot back her last three or four sentences. If you get really good at this, she'll even stop bugging you during the two-minute warning.

Be Good At It. Yes, I mean sex. If you aren't any good—get better! And practice makes perfect! Remember, foreplay is everything to women, and foreplay starts about thirty minutes before actual sex. Flirting with her, teasing her, lighting candles, etc. Not just rubbing her boobs. That only works until you're seventeen.

During sex, slow down. Sex is like beer for men—something to relax you after a long day. But for women it's like champagne. Even if you want to guzzle, let her enjoy the bubbles. Oh, and don't forget the tongue.

Be Creative. Make Her Happy. Bust out the Curly part of your personality. Entertain her. Find some way to make her laugh. Get in the dunk tank at your local carnival. Make up goofy lyrics to the songs on the radio. Cut off your ear and send it to her. That Van Gogh, what a nut!

Surprise her and keep her off guard. Be unpredictable, like when you were just dating. What makes you think she doesn't deserve to be treated like a girlfriend? Remember all that energy you expended getting into her pants? Okay, it won't take that much work, but you have to put some effort in if you want to *stay* in her pants. She's earned it too. Come on, flirt with your girl. The one thing you must avoid is falling into a rut with her. No one likes the same old thing. Out of the blue, take her out on a date—dinner and a movie—or take her to a hotel on a weekend night and order room service. When she shows you her new purse, tell her how great it is. None of your buddies will be there to call you a homo. Drive past the house she was raised in and talk about her childhood. Come home with a gift even though it's not her birthday or one of those Hallmark holidays. Chicks love that sappy shit. (Note: Remember not to refer to any of this as "that sappy shit you love.") And here's a real ace: Let her talk about the relationship.

Respect What She Does. This one is a biggie. And probably the toughest for a guy to remember to do. You need to keep your damn nose out of her areas of expertise. Trust me. It's tougher than it sounds.

We men are used to jumping right in and fixing things, giving advice and taking control of situations. But you have to remember you are part of a "we" now. And think about it. How much does it piss you off at work when you're given an assignment and your boss keeps looking over your shoulder and asking, "How are we doing?" Makes you want to shit in his hard hat, no? Well, you don't want your girl shitting in your hard hat. Especially since, if you're anything like me, you don't quite believe that women do anything as filthy as shitting.

How do you know what is your territory and what is hers? Good question. Here's a guideline:

During one of my divorces I was working with a Teamster named Charlie who told me he had been married for fifty years. At first I thought, "Show-off." But then, after he let me grab a few fries off his plate, I lightened up and asked him what his secret was.

"It's very simple," Charlie said. "When my wife and I started dating, I made it very clear that I was going to make all the big decisions and she could make all the small decisions. That was it.

"She makes all the small decisions. Like what kind of car we're gonna drive, where we're gonna live, how many children we're gonna have, where the kids'll go to school, where we're going on vacation. How we are going to manage the household family from weekly budgets to T-bills."

"Wait a minute." I stopped him. "What are the big decisions?"

"You know, the *big* decisions. Like, should we let China into the UN? Should Ditka come out of retirement? Should Chicago allow a building taller that the Sears Tower? How do we fix the fuckin' Cubs?"

No wonder this guy made it to fifty years! He got it! He let her do her thing, and he did his thing. And how *do* we fix the fuckin' Cubs?

The old dude understood that women are intuitively superior at maintaining the relationship. I used his advice to separate "spheres of influence" in my relationship with Jenny. It goes like this: I'm in charge of the transportation of goods and services. Jenny handles everything else.

In this sense, "goods" implies that it's my job to make sure that anything bigger than a shoebox gets to the house. For example, if we buy a new dishwasher, I'd be responsible for making sure it gets to the house. "Services" means that I manage and coordinate any action that needs to take place to maintain our home. So, to extend the example, I'd also need to make sure that a plumber was there to hook up the dishwasher and that it ran on the correct wiring and plumbing for our kitchen. In short, I coordinate anything that has to do with bringing other men into the house to fix or do things I can't or won't do.

Every now and then I'll see her making an omelet and I'll ask, "Did you add paprika?" Rather than answer, she says, "Is this your territory?"

197

And it's not. So I back down. Then she'll see me struggling to move a new sectional living room set in through the French doors and she'll ask, "Don't you think it'll fit better if you stand it on end?" I simply reply, "Is this your territory?"

And, without a word, she'll leave the room, allowing me to tell the movers I'm paying what I feel is an exorbitant price of ten dollars an hour, to turn the section on its end.

Don't Be a Know-It-All. There's no reason to be an expert on everything. Or, at least, no reason to let her know you are. I'm sure that guy who kept winning on *Jeopardy!* is a nice guy, but who the hell wants that egghead jerk at a party?

You can't be Mr. Know-It-All in a relationship. My buddy Neal is inflicted with expert disease—for good reason. Neal can fix cars, build homes, fly airplanes, pick wines from obscure regions, navigate the toughest rapids on a river raft. He even sailed to Hawaii and back from Los Angeles. Once my wife dropped an earring down the sink. "Call Neal!" she said. "He'll know what to do." The fucker did. I called him and he talked me through dismantling the drain pipe and successfully rescuing the earring. Now any time something goes wrong, Jenny says, "Call Neal!" I'd be pissed off if it didn't get me out of doing a lot of crappy stuff.

But here was the rub: Neal crossed the line with his wife. He fancied himself an expert on child care, house care, "you-name-it" care—and he was. But when his wife would make a mistake, he'd take over that job. He lost trust in her. He treated her like a child. It made her feel worthless, and she acted like a rebellious teenager and left. Part of the work of a relationship is the discipline to keep your mouth shut.

For example, I travel a lot, and I have one of those hanging bags you put sportcoats and shirts in. It was hung up on a hook and my wife was packing for me, but she couldn't find the zipper. In the mirror while I was brushing my teeth, I saw the zipper at the bottom in the corner, with a little flap over it. I bit down hard on the toothbrush and said to myself, "Don't tell her where it is. Don't tell her where it is. Don't tell her where it is. She'll find it." Sure enough, she found the zipper and opened it. It might have taken fifteen seconds longer, and was well worth that time. I didn't look like I was showing "how smart I am" or "how dumb I thought she was." I had to buy a new toothbrush, but that's a lot cheaper than a new wife. Trust me, wives are expensive. You get killed on the trade-in.

Here's another thing women hate: Correcting. Like when she says, "Last Wednesday when we went to the concert . . ." and you interject, "Last Tuesday . . ." Does it really matter? No. So shut up! You hate it when she does it. So don't do it to her! Let her find the zipper when she's ready to find the zipper.

And along the same lines, in a relationship, men have to suppress their desire to "fix." And believe me, buddy, I don't mean stuff around the house. If this relationship does well and you end up getting hitched or living together, you'll be fixing plenty of stuff around the house. I'm talking about fixing problems. Specifically, your lady's problems.

You may hear them say, "I want to be happy, I want to be accepted, I hate that bitch Christie, I want you to listen to me, I want to do yoga, I want you to understand me, I swear my boss is out to get me, I want to be fair, I want to be equal, I don't want to be controlled, I just wish my mother would leave me alone!"

When men hear those kinds of things—and in a relationship, you will hear them over and over again—we start to think, "Is this something I should fix?" Don't fix it! She's just blowing off steam! And I know men want to give a woman what she wants because when *she* feels good, *he* feels good. He fixed something. But that doesn't always solve the problem. Sometimes a woman just wants to be heard and listened to, hugged and cared for. And "fixing" the problem just makes it worse. Be strong enough to not fix it and just listen.

My friend Tony's wife had a dream to work in an art museum. So Tony fixed her problem by moving to an area where there were more museums. Then she wanted to move back near her parents because she wanted to feel a family connection. So they moved. Next she wanted to go on an Outward Bound program, so Tony sent her. But the wilderness was not for her, so he moved her back to the city. Once there, she wanted a baby. A year after the baby was born, she said she felt she was "losing her sense of herself." So she went back to work. Then she wanted to move back to the country because it was the best place to raise kids.

Tony lost his own career because he became a nomad trying to make this woman happy. Sadly, but not surprisingly, she left him because she didn't want to be married any more. He even "fixed" that by giving her the divorce!

Had he listened to me and not started "fixing," she would have worked out her own shit and he'd still be living in his hometown. At very least, he would have held strong to his terms and boundaries and given her something to hold onto in the relationship. Sometimes what a woman says she wants isn't what she really needs. Sometimes she's just testing you. She's testing to see if you're strong enough to deal with her fake bullshit. Because if you're not strong enough to deal with her problems, there's no way you'll be able to handle it if any real problems come along.

And guess what . . . Sometimes there really isn't anything to fix. The problem is just something for your woman to talk about. Women hold onto their problems like their purses. Their problems are like accessories. They help them define themselves to others.

You ever notice how women describe other women when they're not around? It's name first, problem second. "There's Shelley. She and her boss just don't get along." "Have you met Angela? She's trying to become an artist." "Girls, I'm inviting Sylvia to lunch today. Her husband's always trying to 'fix' things." The problem is like a really good purse. It speaks volumes about the woman holding it. Have you ever tried to take a woman's purse away? Or seen how upset she gets when she can't find it? Rip-shit crazy, huh? Now, guess what happens when you "fix" her problem . . . that's right. You've taken away her accessory. Her purse. She'll get pissed and just find a new "purse" anyway. And this time a much bigger one that she can't lose and no one can take away. And watch out for a purse like that!

Last but not least, pick and choose your battles. You know why? Because even if you win these little battles, you'll eventually lose the war. Sure, we all want to have things our way as much as possible, but no one wants to fight and lose over and over again. Not even your girl. The big picture is the relationship, not the little bumps and fights along the way. Remember, you'd rather be wrong than be cooking.

CHAPTER THIRTEEN

THE BEST DEFENSE . . .

I've got an ax-handle pistol with a graveyard frame
That shoot tombstone bullets
Wearin' balls and chain
I'm drinkin' TNT, I'm smokin' dynamite
I hope some screwball start a fight
I'm ready, ready's anybody can be
I'm ready for you, I hope you ready for me

—"I'm Ready," Willie Dixon

Let's slow down for a minute. It's been a few chapters since I've mentioned Simone. She's just sitting outside my office, waiting for me to give her an assignment. In case you've forgotten, Simone is my researcher—my twenty-three-year-old, five-foot-nine dancer-turned-researcher. But that's not why I hired her.

So let's bring her into the discussion, or "rap session," as, I think, people her age still call it. I'll start by asking her a couple of questions. Since I'll have to exit my office, I'll just stop typing, record our conversation into a tape recorder and transcribe it later for the book. [Note: ask agent

re: possible tie-in with/endorsement for RadioShack people—
"Shack up with RadioShack." *Ca-ching!*] And here we go . . .

SOUND OF ME TURNING ON THE TAPE RECORDER.

JIM: . . . fucking red light won't fucking come on. Oh.
Finally.

SOUND OF ME OPENING THE DOOR

JIM: Hey, Simone. Simone, what have I said about smoking inside? Simone? (SOUND OF ME SNAPPING) Earth
to Simone.
SIMONE: Oh, hey. Hi.
JIM: Hi. Simone, what did I say about smoking inside?
SIMONE: Sorry, Mr. B.
JIM: And what did I say about calling me Mr. B? It's Jim,
remember? Call me Jim. I mean, I'm not *that* much
older than you.
SIMONE: Aren't you, like, fift—
JIM: Whoa-hoa, yeah! All right! Anyway, I came out here
because I'm taking a little break from writing and
wanted your feedback on relationships. Y'know, for the
book.
SIMONE: What do you think of my top?
JIM: It's very nice, yes. See, in the book—
SIMONE: Do you like it?

JIM: Yes, sure. It's blue and—oh, it's sheer, look at that. Nice shirt.

SIMONE: I stole it off some drunk girl.

JIM: Good for you.

SIMONE: She was really drunk.

JIM: So you've said. Oh, look. You got a tattoo on your back there. What's it say?

SIMONE: Bone Zone.

JIM: Yep, that's what I thought it said.

SIMONE: Boooooooone Zoooooooone!

JIM: No need to say it again. Back to the book. This chapter I'm doing now is about boundaries—y'know, setting them once you've found a relationship you wanna stick around for. See—

SIMONE: Ohmigod, is that a tape recorder? (INTO TAPE RECORDER) Hello hello hello? (TO ME) This thing records?

JIM: Rumor has it. Simone—

SIMONE: (INTO TAPE RECORDER) Ass. Piss fuck shit shit shit fuck. (LAUGHING)

JIM: Simone, my kids are just down the—

SIMONE: I wanna hear my voice! Play me my voice!

JIM: I'm in the middle of writing. I have a deadline—

SIMONE: Please? Pretty please . . . ? Mr. B . . . ? Jim . . . ?

JIM: All right, just for a second.

SOUND OF ME TURNING OFF TAPE RECORDER, THEN
TURNING IT ON AGAIN.

JIM: . . . in God's name are you crying? Everyone thinks
their voice sounds different on these damn things.
SIMONE: (THROUGH SOBS) I sound like a freak! I'm a
freak! I'm a freak!
JIM: Simone . . . Simone . . . Don't walk away! Where
are you going?
SIMONE: Jacuzzi!
JIM: No, don't—I'll be out in a bit to check on you.

SOUND OF ME TURNING OFF THE TAPE RECORDER.

That didn't go as well as I had hoped. Okay, it was a disaster. Fuckin' Stevie B. Why did I let him talk me into hiring
her? Now I'm bummed. Maybe a dip in the hot tub will
cheer me up.

Ah, very refreshing. My conversation with Simone illustrates two things: (1) how nuts women are and (2) the direct
relationship between keeping a job in this town and owning a see-through top. But back to work:

We've talked (or, to be more accurate, I've written—
you've just sat there like a lazy bastard and read pages all
this time—but, hey, you've paid greenback dollar bills for
these pages so that's your right) on and on and on about the
homework you need to do as a man to keep yourself in line

in a relationship. And all that's important stuff. Real important. But let's face it, it's only half the struggle. There's a whole other half to contend with. The less rational half. The crazier half. That's right, boys . . . the female half.

Keeping yourself in line is the easy part. But how do you keep *her* in line? After all, you've worked your ass off to construct your boundaries. But how do you keep those boundaries safe? Two words: MIND GAMES.

Mind games will keep your young, beautiful girlfriend in check. And the first one I'm gonna tell you right now is the most important. So important it'll need a drumroll . . .

Think of what it was like for you the day you first learned how to walk. Think of the day you first learned how to ride a bike. Think of the day you first learned what you could do with that hole in your pillow (Just me? Okay, moving on). This, friends, is one of those days.

So if you have a trumpet in the house, play it now, son. Play it as loud and as long as you can. Trumpet in the news of perhaps the greatest little piece of knowledge you'll ever learn in your life:

THE BIG TOE THEORY

The Big Toe Theory is based on the idea that when a woman compromises one of your boundaries or terms, or threatens one of the agreements you've made for yourself, you have to respond in such a swift, decisive manner that she'll never do it again. If she puts her "big toe" into your "area," you "hit" that "big toe." I'm using a lot of quotes here, so maybe I should use an example:

Let's say one of the few things you hold dear is watching sports on Sunday. At first, your girl will think it's charming and part of you being a guy. But sooner or later, she will test you to see how strong your resolve is. She'll start dipping her big toe in the proverbial Sports Sunday Pool.

GIRLFRIEND: What are you doing?

YOU: Watching baseball.

GIRLFRIEND: Again? Let's go for a hike.

YOU: Outside?

GIRLFRIEND: Yes. C'mon, it'll be fun.

YOU: Honey, the game's on. C'mon.

GIRLFRIEND: Jesus Christ, there's always a game on. And you're always watching it. When are you going to start making time for me?!

YOU: Never, how do you like that?! And you're goddamn right there's always a game on. You wanna know why? Because baseball season ends one day after you stop bitching about it! It's America's game, damn it! And without it, the good ol' USA would be some shitty, third-world banana republic with watered-down beer and no gadget stores!

A little extreme? Sure, but by doing this, you are letting her know that she should never do this again. You are showing her how dear watching a ball game is to you. Now, you will have to risk a fight over this. And if you end up in a fight, she will accuse you of "hurting" her "feelings." A lesser man would cave right there. But you can't.

You need to come at her with both barrels. Get crazy mad, yell, stomp your feet, throw something, make a scene. The result is that she feels like she was just hit on her big toe with a hammer. You don't want to go too nuts because you're only hitting the toe, not the entire foot, but you need to make your point.

Then, when everything has calmed down, you tell her that she is "everything to you and you don't want to upset her," but this is important to you and she has to respect that. Don't justify or explain and please *don't apologize.*

I'm not saying be mean or abusive, but you must be irrational. If you engage in a reasonable conversation, you are going to lose because women are stronger verbally. By that, I mean you get bored of talking a lot faster than she does and then eventually give in. But if you're a man of action, action will win out. If you allow her toe in your area unchecked, the foot will follow. And if her foot is in your area, it's only a matter of time before she starts storing shoes there. You have to stop her.

Sounds unhealthy, don't it? You're abso-fucking-lutely right it's unhealthy. But if you want a healthy relationship, sometimes you gotta get a little unhealthy. Doesn't make sense? That's why we call these Mind Games.

It's all about keeping your lady off guard. Because if she's off guard, she won't have the time or the desire to get all up in your business. So what else can you do? How can you protect yourself? Keeping this in mind, I introduce a new tactic:

SAY "NO" TO EVERY FOURTH QUESTION

Girls nag. They just do. They're nosy. So out of every four questions that your girlfriend asks you, say "no" to one of them. This will keep her intrigued no matter what the questions are. And if she's guessing, it means you don't fit in the neat little box she thought you fit in. And we've all been in that box—sealed up and packed away in storage. But not anymore. You're mysterious and complex instead of a big, boring idiot. Watch this:

GIRLFRIEND: Honey, will you get my purse?
YOU: Sure.
GIRLFRIEND: Babe, will you bring in the mail?
YOU: Okay.
GIRLFRIEND: Can you get me a glass of water?
YOU: Absolutely.
GIRLFRIEND: Wanna hang up my coat?
YOU: There is no goddamn way I'm getting off my ass to hang up your coat.

All motion will stop at this point, and things might become a little awkward for a few minutes. But you won't be predictable, and you won't become your lady's valet. You've got to throw in a "no" every fourth time because if your wife is batting 1.000, then she's going to tire of the game. This prevents coasting on both parts. Just make sure the fourth question isn't one you really need to say "yes" to.

GIRLFRIEND: Honey, will you get my purse?

YOU: Sure.

GIRLFRIEND: Babe, will you bring in the mail?

YOU: Okay.

GIRLFRIEND: Can you get me a glass of water?

YOU: Absolutely.

GIRLFRIEND: Want a blow job?

YOU: There is no goddamn way I'm—blow job? Yes, please.

"Want a blow job?" Lousy jerks. They always play that card. In that case, you bring the final "no" on the fifth question. Unless . . .

GIRLFRIEND: Honey, will you get my purse?

YOU: Sure.

GIRLFRIEND: Babe, will you bring in the mail?

YOU: Okay.

GIRLFRIEND: Can you get me a glass of water?

YOU: Absolutely.

GIRLFRIEND: Want a blow job?

YOU: There is no goddamn way I'm—blow job?
   Yes, please.

GIRLFRIEND: Do you want me to put on that Catholic
   schoolgirl outfit when I do it?

YOU: No, I—Yes.

GIRLFRIEND: How 'bout I videotape it so you can watch
   it when I'm not around?

YOU: . . . Yes.

GIRLFRIEND: Hey, better still, what if I invite my twin
   sister to join us? She's always had a crush on you.

YOU: Yes! Oh, God, yes!! Whatever you want, baby.

As you can see, this could go on forever. But eventually,
as anyone who's been in a long relationship is fully aware,
the blow job offers stop. And then, when she asks a fourth
question, you can—nay, must—come back with a resound-
ing "no." Remember it keeps them guessing. This leads right
into my next tip:

ONCE IN A WHILE, BE VULNERABLE

I'm not the poster boy for sensitivity. But a tough, stoic man
gets predictable at a certain point. And with predictability
comes boredom. And when women get bored, they stick
their big toe in things. So, to protect myself, once in a while
I throw a sensitivity curveball. I learned this from my
brother.

When I heard the news of my grandmother's death, I was with John. I began crying. "Stop it!" John demanded. "We have to be strong—strong for the women, Jimmy. The women are going to fall apart. We've got to be the soldiers for this family!"

"Okay, okay. I'll be okay," I mustered. And I got my grief out of the way for the funeral. I was a strong young man, following the example of my big, strong brother John. The soldier.

It was a struggle, but at the funeral, I was the portrait of composure. At the reception afterward, I was standing in the back of the room talking to a woman. (No, I wasn't hitting on a cousin at my grandmother's funeral. Okay, maybe I was, but you're missing the point of the story.) All of a sudden, there was a commotion. I turned and saw John bawling uncontrollably as the bishop struggled to hold his convulsing body up. The woman I was talking to immediately rushed over to console him. Every woman there was doting on John the rest of the day: "Oh, Johnny, oh, Johnny, don't cry." Soldier, my ass.

As I watched this scene, I remembered a time when I was driving with him and he dropped food on his shirt. I told him I'd take him home to change, but he said, "No. It makes me vulnerable. The most vulnerable person in any scene wins the scene because vulnerability is the most honest moment." John wasn't deliberately trying to hog all the attention (at least . . . I don't *think* he was). He just couldn't remain stoic any longer. And once he broke, he was the most honest person in the moment.

The best way to endear yourself to a girl is to be vulnerable. *The most vulnerable person in the room always wins.* That's why women always have the advantage in an argument. They can cry at the drop of a hat. Arguing with someone who's crying makes you feel like crap and you start to cave.

Once in a while, be vulnerable. It works. They won't know what hit them. And they'll be so touched and so off guard with their new sensitive man, they'll never think about stepping into your space. And if you really want to see a woman off guard, here's a great mind game:

FINGER IN THE BUTT

Or . . .

FAKE JEALOUSY

Our old friend Stevie B. taught me how important the tool of jealousy could be in a relationship, and I still use it to this day. One day Jenny and I were taking a walk and we passed a construction site. Jenny said hello to a bricklayer on the scaffolding and commented on what a great job he was doing, because she's the nicest person in the whole world. I smelled an opportunity for a mind game. Because I'm *not* the nicest person in the world.

We walked for several more blocks, but I didn't say

a word, just furrowed my brow. It took her a while to notice, because she does most of the talking. But when she did, she asked if anything was wrong. "Nothing . . . I don't want to talk about it." She asked again, and I curtly repeated myself.

Stevie B. says that every four to six weeks, a man has to get fake stupid crazy jealous to keep his girlfriend from thinking he is taking her for granted. Furrow your brow, grind your teeth, and breathe heavily through your nose. You can try this, or pick your own similarly convincing tic. Just be ridiculous . . . the same as The Big Toe Theory.

When we walked into the house, I stormed across the room, grabbed a plastic coffee mug and smashed it on the kitchen floor. (Stevie B. told me to break something, but to make sure it was inexpensive.) Then I started my tirade.

ME: I saw the way you looked at that bricklayer!
THE LOVELY MRS. BELUSHI: What?

(I had her attention, so I turned up the volume.)

ME: You heard me! You want him, don't you?! Don't you!
THE LOVELY MRS. BELUSHI: Are you crazy?

(I find that the best way to sustain a tirade is to repeat whatever the chick says, but louder.)

ME: Crazy? You're damn right I'm crazy! You practically dragged him into the porta-john to blow him.
THE LOVELY MRS. BELUSHI: Omigod, calm down. You're not making any sense.

ME: You're goddamn right I'm not making any sense!

THE LOVELY MRS. BELUSHI: I can't talk to you when you're like this. I'll talk to you tomorrow.

ME: Tomorrow?! Tomorrow?! TOMORROW???!!!

Three "tomorrows." Nice touch, don't you think? My improv background at work; please hold your applause.

The next day I heard Jenny on the phone talking to one of her girlfriends. She was telling her how much her man loves her and how insanely jealous he got last night. When she hung up I asked her who she was talking to. "The bricklayer," she responded. She was letting me coyly know that she was all mine and I shouldn't worry my crazy self about the bricklayer. And then I got cake. See, flowers and a note are nice, but pounding your chest really shows your girlfriend how much you care in a distinctly caveman way.

There's one last thing I want to bring up on this subject. Sure I've given you a lot of great advice. And if you use it, you should be in pretty good shape. But let's say it doesn't work. What if you're new to sticking up for yourself and all of my mind games and boundary-protecting backfire? If this happens, dear readers, I offer this fail-safe plan:

DON'T BE AFRAID TO ASK A DUDE FOR HELP

Here's a little Hollywood story that illustrates my point. At the time of one of my impending marriages, I was working on Michael Mann's first feature film, *Thief.* My fiancée and I were supposed to get married on my day off. Two days before the wedding, Mann (the Mike Ditka of filmmakers) came to me to tell me that due to a last-minute scheduling snafu, he needed me to work on Saturday. This, as it turned out, was also supposed to be my wedding day.

"Michael," I told him, "I can't tell my girl to cancel the wedding because you need to shoot a scene." There was a long pause. Mr. Mann stared at me, so I bluffed.

"If you need the shot so bad, call my bride-to-be and you tell her she has to reschedule the day that she's dreamt about since she was five." There was another long pause and a longer stare. This guy knew how to work the silences.

He grabbed the phone. "What's her number?" he asked. He dialed with confidence and purpose. I was tense.

I heard his half of the conversation: "Hi, this is Michael Mann. How are you? . . . Oh, thank you . . . Jim's doing a terrific job on the movie. Listen, I'm going to need him this Saturday . . . Great, thank you so much." He hung up the phone, turned to me and said, "You're working on Saturday." Shit, now that's a real man. He didn't even say "I'm sorry" to her.

My job was saved. My wedding was saved (which was good, because you always want your first wedding to go well). And all because I wasn't afraid to ask a guy for a little help. Actually it was more that I was too afraid of Mr. Mann to say no, so I bluffed him, but either way it worked out.

Except that the marriage ended in divorce and Mann never hired me again.

Remember when I told you that if you show your wounds to a man you'll have a brother, but show your wounds to a woman and you'll have a mother. No? Why the fuck not! That was some poignant shit. It even rhymes.

But surely you remember that you need a community of men that you can lean on for support. Unless you skimmed over the first hundred friggin' pages! Well, now that you're in a committed relationship, it doesn't mean it's time to kick those guys to the curb. Quite the opposite. Now is when you need to make sure you have them around. You need an outlet to express your fears and concerns. Women say they want you to share this stuff with them, but they don't.

Ever date a girl for a couple weeks and casually mention you were thinking it might be fun to take her on a little weekend trip to a cabin your buddy lets you use in the summer? You know, when you sorta make a plan with a girl that's farther into the future then the amount of time you've actually been together? I bet you that you didn't take her on that trip. Know why? Because you freaked her out and she dumped you. You scared her. By planning that far out you are assuming she'll be around that long. That you *need* her to be around that long.

If you choose to share your darkest fears, your wounds, with your girlfriend, she will listen to you. And she'll *sound* supportive and loving. But inside, you've scared the shit out of her. And once you scare her she'll start to doubt and mistrust you. Once she mistrusts you, she'll start getting pissed at you. Women want men to be rocks. Doesn't she deserve a strong man who can handle his shit? Not some whiny schoolboy who needs her to hold his hand because the world is so tough.

Once you put her in the position of having to be *your* protector, she'll start punishing you. And she'll keep punishing you until the relationship can't take it any more and it ends. Then she'll punish you for a little while after that for safe measure. Trust. It's delicate. You have to work to keep it, because it's hell to get it back.

But we're not able to live without fear. So the key is to *appear* to be a rock. The only way to do that is to find another outlet to express your fears. That's what your dudes are for.

Don't trick yourself into thinking, or hoping, that if you teach her a lesson once, she'll remember it forever. These techniques are vitamins, not vaccinations. Or, to paraphrase a great man: You got miles to go before you sleep, pal. You know who said that? Jesus. [Simone?—JB]

Before I send you off into the next chapter, I have to first tell you of a tragedy that befell the Belushi house as I was writing these last pages—Simone's boyfriend came to the house today. You remember Simone, right? My twenty-three-year-old, five-foot-nine dancer-turned-researcher. But that's not why I hired her.

What's that? You're surprised to hear that she had a boyfriend? Well, so was I when I met him! Actually, I didn't really meet him. I just heard him lay on his horn from my driveway and shout, "Hey, Tits! Get the lead out!"

Dion, as I later found his name to be, was here to pick up Simone after work. And with a smile on her face and a quick "Knockin' off early, Mr. B.!" she was out the door. Even though it *was* only noon, she *had* been at my house proof-reading for a full forty-five minutes, so I figured I had cracked the whip enough for one day and let her leave.

After she left, you can guess my reaction. I was crushed. Look, I am happily married and would never do anything untoward with Simone, but I had been operating under the assumption that she had some creepy quasi-stalkerish at-tachment to me. Frankly, thinking she got a charge from just being around me made it easier in my mind to pay her as little as I did. But it was all based on a lie. She didn't har-bor a secret crush on me. She didn't have a shrine of photos of me over her bed. She was actually dating someone.

Why didn't she tell me she had a boyfriend? Because she forgot? Nope. Because she's stupid? She is, but that's not the reason. What's that you say? Because she's a filthy tease who knew her imaginary availability is the only currency she has in this bankrupt town? Well, you said it, not me, okay?

For all her incompetence in the world of proofreading and researching, Simone knew exactly what she was doing. But I can't blame her. She's a woman. And that's what women do. They identify the strengths they have and use them. They manipulate. And because of this, right now Simone is laughing at me, as Dion is repeatedly, and presumably without protection, befouling her "bone zone."

But I can't fire her now, can I? After all, it would be a real pain in the ass to hire someone new so late in the game. And she does drop your jaw when she's wearing a bikini. So dealing with Simone on this is not the best way to go. That leaves me with Dion.

Dion. It's go time.

As you can see, like all men, I'm weak when it comes to a pretty lady. That's something you and I have in common. What we don't have in common, dear reader, is I have Governor Schwarzenegger's personal cell phone number in my Rolodex. One call to my fellow *Red Heat* star and good ol' Dion (Lic.# 5TYH982—oh, yeah, Mr. B.'s got videocams in the driveway) is visited by thirty cops outside his Reseda apartment. Let's make the charge be, say, graft. Yeah, that'll do. Abracadabra, no more Dion. Thank you, Governator.

Booooooooone Zooooooooone!

CHAPTER FOURTEEN

SHACKING UP

Hey pretty baby
Do you remember when I first came knockin' on your
front door
I think about it and it makes me laugh
I can see your face like a photograph
You looked at me like "I don't know"
I smiled and said "Well, here we go."
Bless my soul
Looks like we're on a roll

—"Bless My Soul," Glen Clark

You've managed to get out of the way of your own natural tendencies just long enough to establish a healthy, stable, loving relationship. Through diligent care for your boundaries and strict adherence to the principles I have set forth for you, you have a great woman in love with you.

This is where the chick movies usually fade out. I know you've never seen any of them. Neither have I. But I've starred in some of them, so trust me when I say the movies always end with the happy couple realizing they are meant to be together. You know why it fades out there? Because that's when it starts to get boring.

Once you've locked in your partner, things can get stale. Relationships are about motivation, however, so you have to keep things moving.

Fifty years ago, when you reached this stage of the relationship there was only one option: Marry the girl, have three kids, work until you retire and die in Florida. It's not a bad life, but the days of *Our Town* have long passed. Just because you get along with someone doesn't mean that you are ready to propose. You see, nowadays the goal is not just to get married, but to get married to someone you aren't going to divorce. It's a tall order, believe me—I know! But it can be done.

Like I said, fifty years ago it was different, but those people lived through the Depression and World War II. Do you think you could have lived through that shit? I didn't think so. See, they had a higher threshold for suffering. Once you've had boiled boot soup for dinner, staying married to an asshole is easy.

That generation was so tough that it left their offspring little place to go except therapy. The result was a generation of long-haired, peace-lovin', drug-takin', war-protestin', veggie-eatin', rock-'n'-roll-listenin', hippie-dippie beatnik freaks. In short, the world got a lot less uptight. For example, in just thirty years being risqué went from not wearing a bra to getting your clit pierced. It's a little something we historians call the sexual revolution.

Men usually focus on the upside of the sexual revolution: i.e., multiple partners. But there was a price: i.e., having to work on relationships. Somewhere in all the focus on feelings, women started to look for partners rather than providers. And men started to look for lovers rather than maids. Basically, the institution of marriage became defined by something it was never meant to embody—romance.

Like marriage, the courtship ritual changed as well. Suddenly, you had to actually get to know one another and see if your mate was compatible with you, as opposed to simply not repulsed by you. The biggest change to courtship is that there is now an additional step between getting serious with a girl and getting engaged. It's called living together.

Hey! Hey! You pick this book up right now! Goddamnit, get back here! Do not freak out. Get a paper bag and take some deep breaths in it. You can handle this. Are we calm? Okay, good. I'll continue. Just keep that bag handy.

Now it used to be that "cohabitation" was considered "living in sin" and was shunned by the general population. In fact, it's still technically illegal for an unmarried, unrelated man and woman to live together in some states. Ironically, many of these states are the same ones where it's legal to be married *and* related. I only bring this up because there's an ethical consideration here. For some guys it's okay to have premarital sex, but moving in with a woman is taboo. Mental health professionals refer to this condition as "Scared of your Mommy."

It is just a simple fact of life that your parents are going to cluck their tongues and roll their eyes if you tell them you plan to shack up with a chick. This is assuming that they don't threaten to tan your behind with a belt. While it's not true of all parents, you should be prepared for it. Keep in mind that this is a good thing. If you can't stand up to your parents, then perhaps the only woman you should be shacking up with is . . . Mommy.

But keep in mind that your parents are probably bitter because they know if they had gotten to live with their spouse for six months before the wedding, they would have realized what a horrible mistake they were making.

Moral qualms aside, it's also a big deal for a guy. Remember talking about Saddam's spider hole? That's a guy's idea of a living space. You move in with a woman and suddenly your "place" becomes your "home."

Seriously, dude, I am gonna get bored if you keep throwing the book down. Pick it up. Come on. Good. Okay, I know you don't want to hear all this, but you can hear it from me, or you can let her dictate the terms.

Let's start by talking about how you know you're ready to move in together. Now you've already done the work I laid out for you in the previous chapters and that's all going well. So well, in fact, that you two are seeing a lot of each other. Inevitably, you wind up crashing at her place. Here are the stages:

Stage one: *The Walk of Shame.* This gets its name from the college tradition of sorority girls who have to stumble home on a Sunday morning still wearing the little black cocktail dress from the night before. Now, it means you knew you'd end up at her place, but didn't want to look like you were expecting anything. You wake up and slide into the clothes from the night before and drive home to shower before you have to get to work.

Stage two: *Meet Your Second Toothbrush.* She buys you a toothbrush and gives it to you to keep at her house. It means you're going to wake up there. You also give her a toothbrush to keep at your place. Actually, she buys it. You don't know where to buy toothbrushes.

Stage three: *The "I Totally Got Some" Bag.* You bring a spare set of clothes in an overnight bag on your date so that you can shower and change at her place the following morning. This saves you a trip home before work. You might even accidentally leave it on the front seat of your car so that your coworkers know that you totally got some.

Stage four: *The Drawer.* Capturing a piece of a woman's heart is child's play compared to getting her to partition some of her fashion storage space. She allows you to keep a small amount of clothing at her place in a drawer or part of her closet. This means that you will not have to plan when you crash there, but it also means that you will have to keep it stocked with fresh underwear, socks, etc. In theory, this should make things easier, but ultimately it means you are now keeping inventory of two sets of laundry.

Stage five: *Extreme Makeover: Spider-hole Edition.* Constantly waking up at her place to discover that "The Drawer" only has one clean sock for you to wear to work has given you the idea that it would be easier if she crashed at your place more often. You both agree this is a good idea, but your place grosses her out and, truth be told, you're not really proud enough of the pad to have her over. To fix this, you set out to give your apartment or house a cleaning the likes of which it's never seen before. Maybe you even buy furniture so she doesn't have to sit on a beanbag when she comes. She probably even crashes there once or twice before the normal layer of filth resettles.

Stage six: *Lost.* You get in your car after work and have to think about which way to turn out of the parking garage, because you can't remember if you're going to her place or yours. You have two places you call home, but you are somehow ultimately homeless. [Simone, see if I can get some kind of product placement money from ABC for using two of their show titles in this chapter. Maybe I could re-name the "I Totally Got Some" Bag to "George Lopez's 'You totally got lucky last night' bag of fun"—JB]

Eventually you want to go back to having just one toothbrush and all your socks at a common location. The easiest way to accomplish this is to dump her. Not biting? Okay, then you have only one option. And you better not throw the book down again.

I mean it.

So you've decided to move in with your girlfriend. You could view this as simply a living arrangement to better facilitate dating her. If you're Catholic, you could view this as a way to guarantee swift passage to Hell when you die. Or you could look at this as a chance to gather valuable intelligence about this woman before you decide to marry her.

Pick the book up. Come on, dude. All I said was "marry." It's just a word. You aren't locked in to it yet.

LIVING IN SIN—IS SHE WIFE MATERIAL?

That's how I propose you start thinking of her. Note that I said "thinking" of her. Do not refer to her as your "potential wife" out loud. Just get it in your head that this is an audition period for her. Make no mistake, you're trying out for "potential husband," but let's have her worry about that.

Before you move in—I can't stress this enough—*have a plan.* My suggestion is that you move in with her for a year. By the end of that year, you will decide whether this is someone you are ready to marry. Maybe you say this out loud to her, maybe you don't. The point is to have a firm plan. I know you did this as a half measure to avoid a more serious commitment, because once you live together, inertia will keep you together unless you are motivated. Have an exit strategy, or your home will become a quagmire.

I just won fifty bucks from Stevie B. He said there was no way I could work the word "quagmire" into this book.

The first big decision you will have to make is where you are going to live. Now, I don't know you. Maybe you rent an apartment, maybe you own a home, maybe you both have roommates, maybe one of you has pets. I don't know any of this stuff about you. Here's what I do know: She's going to suggest you move into her place.

It's going to make a lot of sense to you, too. I mean, her place is nicer, better kept up, and you two are both used to it. You'll think that's a good idea. And it'll be so easy.

THIS IS ONE OF THOSE PARAGRAPHS YOU SHOULDN'T SKIM OVER!

Never. Give up. Home. Field. Advantage. Never. I don't care where she lives. It's always going to be *her* place.

I cite the case of the New York Jets, a fine NFL franchise from the nation's largest city that has seen Hall of Fame players and coaches over the years. They even hold the distinction of being the first AFL team to win a Super Bowl when Broadway Joe Namath's prediction came true. It was a great day for the Jets. And the last great day. The Jets have become perennial underachievers, chokers or just plain losers. How could a team from such a huge media market toil in futility for so long? The answer is simple: They have no home games.

The New York Jets play their non–away games at a place called Giants Stadium. You may have heard of the place because it's the stadium the New York Giants play their home games in.

How are the Jets ever going to be their own team if they have to park under a huge sign for another team when they go to work? The same is true for you, my friend. You can change her place to make it more hospitable to you, but it's always going to be hers. That means there are going to be landmines that have been lying there for years that you had no idea about.

Say you've lived there for a month. One day you decide you want toast for breakfast and you're surprised to learn that the toaster isn't plugged in. You find an outlet, connect the toaster and pop a couple pieces of whole wheat in to be made warm and good. Oh yeah, dude. It's gonna be whole wheat. You're living with a chick now.

Suddenly the lights go out and the coffeemaker stops. She comes storming into the kitchen in a towel (she was in the shower). She quickly realizes what's happened and starts clucking her tongue at you. You plugged the toaster into the rice cooker outlet. You have to use the plug on the other wall or else it'll blow a fuse because of the hot water maker and the fridge. It's a simple system and she's happy to show you how it all works . . . but she'll always, always be the boss.

"Honey, we keep the dish towels under the sink. These are the hand towels for the bathroom." "Dear, we squeegee the shower door right after we get out so it doesn't spot." "Oh, I'm sorry, but would you mind putting on pants if you're going to sit there." Everywhere you turn there will be rules, and you will be breaking them.

The only way to make living together work is to move her into your place or find a new place together. Either way, it's essentially a neutral field. You've never paid attention to your place the way she will, so it will change, but it will be yours first, and that will give you a leg to stand on. If you move into a new place together, at least you'll get to watch the nesting process take place, so you'll know what's important to her and why.

Once you pick a place to live, you'll have to begin the moving. I'm telling you right now, do not bother packing. If you put all your stuff in boxes and move it to the new place, you will have wasted a day of your life. Take your potential wife to your place and go through your stuff before you pack it. This stage is what I call:

LETTING GO OF YOUR CRAPPY STUFF

The stuff your potential wife has in her house was picked for reasons like decorating schemes, functionality, the amount of light in the room, etc. In essence, she has reasons for owning her stuff. Men collect things the way a snowball hurtling downhill picks up snow—based solely on what crosses our path. Now that you are living with a woman, you have to think about what is nice, rather than what is cool.

If you allow her to review your stuff, you'll have 95% less stuff to move. This is a hard process for most men. It may have taken you years to steal all the milk crates you keep your DVDs in. Your friends have often noted with envy the condition of your complete set of *The Fast and the Furious* collector plastic mugs from Arby's. And the stains on your futon represent a lot of memories to you.

You have every right to fight her on some of this stuff. But you will lose, and frankly, you should. Your inflatable lawn chair featuring the members of KISS is pretty cool, but you've outgrown it, even if you think you haven't. If she says something is too tacky, rundown or ridiculous to have in your new space, she's right. The simple fact is that you aren't qualified to make that determination.

I have two German Shepherds who regularly drag dead birds and squirrels into the house. In their minds, it makes perfect sense that we would keep a crow's neck in the living room. When you tell your potential wife you really want to put your Chicago Bears Helmet Phone in the kitchen, you are just as wrong as Chooch and Truly.

You are only allowed to put your foot down on things that have significant sentimental value to you and can be displayed tastefully or put in storage. "Stairway to Heaven" is the greatest song of all time, but I don't care how you frame a poster version of the lyrics, it ain't gonna be tasteful. Garages were invented to hide men's shit.

Speaking of hiding stuff, there is an important distinction to be made when it comes to evaluating your stuff. Your potential wife's judgment of what goes and what stays should not and cannot extend to your porn collection. I know, I know. You don't have anything like that. Let's just pretend you do for a moment.

The first thing you have to do is pare it down to the greatest hits. I know this stash has kept you going through some rough times. Understandably, you have grown attached.

After all, you've had more intimate relationships with some of these magazines and videos than with women you've dated for months. But the truth is, the more you bring with you, the more you risk having it uncovered.

Once you eliminate the bulk of the material, find a place you know is safe. If you have any doubts about it, give yourself an insurance policy. For example, if it's in your closet, mention that you thought you saw a mouse in there. Her fear might not overwhelm her curiosity, but it'll slow her down.

I also propose that you have a safety stash that you don't hide as well. Something like *Maxim* or *Playboy* that lets her know that you do have porn, but leaves her thinking it's not as demented as it really is. Finding the safety stash will keep her from looking further. The difference is when she finds the safety stash, she'll be shocked. Trust me, that's better than appalled, which is what she'd be if she found your regular stash.

I'm not some out-of-date old dude, either. I know that for a lot of you, this stash might only exist on a computer. Don't think for one second this makes you safe. Even the most technologically challenged woman has a friend who does computer consulting work at some big accounting firm. Sooner or later they'll go out for tea and the computer chick will tell your potential wife all the ways to find out what sites you've been visiting. Ironically, the whole time she was out for tea, you were at home surfing boobs.com.

Be aware of your cookie and your history, as well as

where all the files are. If you aren't technologically savvy enough to know what the hell I'm talking about, you better make friends with a nerd and learn how to cover your tracks.

It's not enough that you just clear your cookie out. You have to fill it up with shit to explain why you were up for four hours after she went to bed. After you clear it out, go to ESPN.com and check some scores. That way she'll just think you're a meathead sports fan and not the sick pervert you are.

Maybe you're one of those guys who doesn't like porn. I've read about you in science journals, but never met you. The bottom line is that guys require a certain amount of . . . shall we say "maintenance?" It's not like girls never maintain themselves, but let's be real. It's nowhere near the same frequency. She might think that she's not satisfying all your needs sexually. Truthfully, that is the case. But an entire cheerleading squad hopped up on coke could probably only keep up with your full sexual needs for a week or two.

This leads me to an important, but often overlooked piece of advice: Make sure there's a lock on the bathroom door. There are two things you don't want to be in the middle of when she walks in: 1) "awakening the giant" and 2) "growing a tail." Frankly, no one wants to see you growing a tail, but that's just part of maintaining boundaries once you move in. The truth is, you are going to eventually see more of one another than you are used to, but you have to keep some things behind the curtain. You can't let her see you awakening the giant.

Imagine, if you will, one day coming home and finding your potential wife in bed exploring the Batcave. What would your reaction be? That's right, you'd be unbelievably turned on. That's in proportion to how turned off she'd be if she caught you. So you need to be careful. Not because you're scared. Because you're courteous.

Why am I putting so much emphasis on allowing for alone time with yourself? Why should you worry about that now that you are going to have your own in-house supply of booty? Okay, you're going to want to throw the book down again, but what I'm going to say is both important and true.

Once you move in and get all comfortable together, the amount of sex you have is going to taper off.

True, this is not what you signed up for, but be prepared for it. And know that it won't all be because of her. You will also find that you aren't as interested as you once were.

More important than the frequency, however, is the way you are going to have sex. When you first sleep with a girl, you try a little harder, don't you? Guess what, so does she. Eventually, you'll both feel you don't need to impress one another.

Ask a woman about oral sex. They'll have lots to say. Then say, "No, I meant blow jobs," and suddenly they are less interested. They all say it takes too long to satisfy the guy. Course, when they were dating you, they were motivated to bob up and down on that lollipop. But now that you're living there, all a blow job means to them is a stiff neck.

When you were first dating, she liked the way you looked naked; now she wonders if you were always so hairy. She used to enjoy foreplay, but now she says things like, "If we have sex, will you not touch me for the next twenty-four hours?" They start using sex as a negotiating tool. If you buy into this, you are going to negotiate yourself out of having sex and right out of the relationship.

First things first: If you haven't gotten laid for a year, get out now! You are not going to get laid for the next three. I'm not kidding. I have so many married friends who haven't gotten laid for two years and stuck around for two more years. Their wife has bullshitted them into believing that she has some kind of "problem." ("I'm feeling heavy right now." "I don't feel sexy.") Oh yeah, guys, there's a problem! You—for buying that bullshit.

If it's less than a year, what do you do? Drop a pack of matches somewhere discreet in the bedroom. Make sure the matches have a girl's name and phone number written on the back. Nothing will get you head faster than a making a woman think you're considering cheating on her. Not only will you get laid . . . you'll get her "A" game.

But before all that, you have to be honest. You have to be clear that regular sexual encounters are something you expect. At the same time, know that it's not going to be a honeymoon forever. When things taper off, you'll be glad you hid that stash.

Now, if you are like most men, you won't be totally

locked out like some bad hockey strike. You just won't get laid a lot, and you'll walk around complaining to your guy friends about the lack of sex. Sample dialogue: "Dude, gettin' any?" "Nah, you?" "Nope."

If you find this is happening, remember that you need to flirt with your potential wife. Tell her how nice she smells. Always compliment her hair. Boost her ego whenever you can. A great tip is to compliment her shoes. Women will always love hearing about their shoes. No matter what body image issues a woman has, young or old, from the ankles down, they can always look like Angelina Jolie. You must flatter or flirt with her every single day. It only takes three minutes, and if you do it in front of someone, it doubles the impact.

Last summer, I was at a party with my wife. Right in front of a group of women I put both hands on her ass, squeezed and declared loud enough for some of the women to hear: "You've got the best ass!" (Notice I said "ass," adding just an edge of crudity to ensure that people would look up.) Jenny pulled back, but the women sitting in the vicinity were clearly impressed that I was hot for my wife. And that made Jenny feel sexy. That wasn't even three minutes; it was thirty seconds. But you can't do that too often. Newton's law of averages says you'll eventually grab the wrong ass.

The bottom line is that your woman deserves the same flirting you give to every secretary you pass in the hallway at work or barista making your coffee. You're going to see a lot of one another, and the more you utilize those moments, the more benefits you can receive. You can't flirt with someone all day every day, but just do it a little more than you want to. Fight your urge to be lazy, and she'll pay you back in spades.

But perhaps the biggest key to living together is figuring out ways to be apart. Here's the get-down: A MAN NEEDS HIS OWN TERRITORY. That is a universal term that applies to men of every species. Tomcats spray everywhere, marking their territory. A male dog takes a leak on each and every tree in the neighborhood during a walk. Monkeys jerk off constantly. I don't know if this is to mark their territory, but it sure must be for something important.

Take as an example the most legendary and iconic figure of twentieth century literature: Superman. (You were afraid I meant real literature, weren't you?) The strongest man alive, able to look through concrete walls (but discreet enough not to check out Lois Lane's sweater), champion of truth, justice and the American way, Superman is, quite simply, the guy every guy wants to be. Why is that? Because he's so moral and good? Because he can fly? Because the ladies dig him? No.

Every guy wants to be Superman because he has the Fortress of Solitude. A giant palace that is in a remote location so inhospitable to human life that only *he* can get there. What does Superman do in the Fortress of Solitude?

I have no idea. The point is that even the mightiest, most noble man in the universe occasionally just has to get the fuck away from everyone.

HAVE A FORTRESS OF SOLITUDE

I once knew a married couple who fought constantly. I asked them what was going on in their relationship, and I realized that this guy didn't have his Fortress of Solitude. And with the controlling piece-of-work he was married to, he definitely needed some solitude. I suggested that they assign a part of the house to be his and his alone. They tried it out and, you know what? They fought a lot less.

Find a spot that is yours and yours alone. Perhaps it's a shed in the backyard or a garage. Don't have that much room? It can be a dirty corner in the basement with a smelly drain in the floor. Have your own spot. A place that is your personal spider hole that you can go to, no questions asked. And defend that turf with your life. No one can enter unless invited. If it's not available to us, we will feel on edge and eventually we'll push her out of our shared spaces so that we can get our dose of solitude.

I like to compare it to my two German Shepherds. When they sleep, they always have one ear up listening for trouble. They never truly rest, because they are on guard. But if I put them in their crate and lock the door, they know they can't defend anything and they sleep completely. That's the relaxation a guy gets in his own space. There's a corollary to this one.

BE A GOOD GUEST

Let her have privacy, too. Don't invade her space. The worst offense is asking what she was doing last night when she wasn't with you, even if it is tearing up your insides. Trust me, you don't want to know. It's either too boring or too wild. Book club or strip club. Either way, it's none of your damn business. You worry about your territory.

Being a good guest does not apply specifically to the space you're living in. A. Justin Sterling proposes that men need to think of themselves as being a good guest in the *re-lationship.* Remember when you were a kid and your mom took you to Aunt Patty's? You loved her cookies, so you were always excited to go there. You knew you had to be on your best behavior, though, or you'd never get asked back. You wiped your feet before you entered. You didn't splash on the bathroom mirror when you washed your hands. You always used a coaster for your sodas. You knew to act like you knew Aunt Patty would want you to. Be the same way in your re-lationship and, I promise you, you'll get your cookie.

When a husband passes away and they ask the widow what he was like she says he was kind, thoughtful, generous, sensitive. A great man. That's called the widow's list.

Typically, women describe all *living* men as ungrateful, thoughtless, sloppy, lazy, rude. A doofus. The key is to behave in such a way so that your potential wife describes you to her friends as if she's a widow. I know that sounds fucked up, but it's just a simple human truth that it's easier to like dead people.

But there are going to be spaces you two have to share. I'm talking about closet space, medicine cabinet space, your side of the bed, etc. This is where you need to be in your goal-line defense.

I remember visiting my cousin Gus shortly after he was married. "Look at this!" he said, pointing into their bedroom closet. He put his index finger on the support bar for the pole. "This is the center of the closet. What do you see on the right side?"

". . . a skirt and blouse . . ."

"Aha!" he said, shaking his index finger at the pole. "She knows from this point to the right is mine and from this point to the left is hers. She's intruding on my space."

"Gus, it's three hangers," I reasoned.

"Last week it was one! This is an escalation. It's how Saddam took Kuwait, you know."

"Gus," I said, "calm down. We got Kuwait back."

"That's what she said, big surprise there. So I say, 'I keep my shit on my side of the closet, you need to keep your shit on your side!'"

Truth be told, Gus had about eight shirts and her side was crammed to the gills, but his point was well taken. He had claimed his territory and she was challenging his sovereignty without formal negotiations. If she had asked to spill over to his side, he probably wouldn't have hesitated to yield the space. But if he let it go unchecked, she'd in essence have an easement that allowed her to creep past the centerline.

Plus there was precedent to consider. How could Gus let this go and then have any kind of legal leg to stand on when her cosmetics annexed his side of the bathroom sink? Women are beautiful creatures, but they spread like viruses. (I have the sinking feeling this is the quote the National Organization for Women is going to pull to condemn this book. But I kept it in, just so they'd have to read this far.)

There are, however, many spaces that won't be your territory or hers. These shared spaces need to be maintained, and figuring out who does what is an important process. When you do this, remember one thing: She is always going to think she does all the work.

The reason for this is simple: She'll do all the work. I mean, you'll chip in. But as is evidenced by the shithole you are currently living in, maintaining the home just isn't as important to you. There are chores she does that you won't even know existed. Did you know some clothes can't go in the dryer? Seriously.

The important thing is that you make the effort to do some of the work. If there is a task you find particularly taxing, try to do a really crappy job at it. Eventually, she'll get sick of redoing your work and take over that responsibility entirely. Now you don't want to wind up in a place where your only "chore" is to lift your feet when she vacuums around you. Make sure there is at least one honest-to-goodness task you perform for every ten she does.

It's important at this point to think of a theory which my friend David Deida calls "polarity." Human beings exist in a spectrum that goes from Masculine to Feminine. The separation of these two "poles" creates attraction. The best example of this is a battery. As a relationship has a male and a female partner, a battery has a positive and a negative pole. These two poles are attracted to one another. They move towards one another and create electrical current. But as they rush together they start to co-mingle. Once this happens the attraction wanes. Eventually positive and negative are equally distributed and your car won't start.

That example might have no basis in actual science, but the point is, there has to be a separation between your essence and your girlfriend's. The more masculine you are, the more feminine she's *allowed* to be. It's the same reason why she was secretly looking for Tony Soprano when you were dating. There's a troubling and persistent myth these days that a "modern man and woman" should be equal and balanced. When that happens the man becomes less distinctly male and takes on feminine qualities. The inverse happens to the woman. Maybe it's the converse, I never understood those fucking words, but you get my point. Equal and balanced ends up with two people that are essentially the same. When that occurs you'll become best friends, business partners and roommates. And then, eventually, she'll become someone you never want to fuck again. You've lost your polarity so there's no electricity between the poles. You need the electricity for the spark.

There is one chore that is not only your responsibility, it is your duty. Every night when you two go to bed, it is your job to make sure the door is locked. This defines you as protector of the realm. It also means you have to get out of bed and check it out every time she thinks she hears a serial-killer/rapist breaking in, but it beats washing dishes.

You are also going to have to discover a new understanding of economics. Women have a very different relationship with money than we do. My theory is that it's all based around the fact that they never have to pay for drinks.

The point is that now that you're living together, you can't spend every day like it's a big date for which you pick up the check. You both have to contribute to the household pot. The catch is that you're used to having shithead roommates that you just split everything evenly with. That isn't going to fly anymore. You have to base what you each pay on what you each make. For example, if you make three times as much as her, you should pay three times as much as she does for expenses. If she makes four times as much as you . . . well, good job, dude.

You also have to nail down what you both consider shared expenses. Food and rent are obvious, but what if she wants to buy a rug? Are toiletries included? Toilet paper is one thing, but a seventy-dollar tube of mousse? The only way to make it work is to sit down and talk about it all.

Don't get bent out of shape trying to make things fair and equal. I don't think the words "fair and equal" have any place in a relationship. They're too hard-line. Stuff you'd find in a contract. And relationships shouldn't be that "letter of the law." That's why you don't need a lawyer to start dating, just to get divorced. And nobody has fun during a divorce. "Fair and equal" are completely subjective terms. If your girlfriend tells you she doesn't feel "equal," what are you supposed to say? If you say she is equal it means you are discounting her feelings. If you say she isn't equal then you are "holding her down." When those words get pulled out in an argument, men take on the look of a deer in the headlights. They can't see any escape path.

Instead of using fair and equal, I like to use "what works" and "what's equitable." Women are smaller, yet they take up more of the bed than men. How fair is that? Not very. But does it work? You bet. So be flexible. I sleep on a narrow strip of the bed, and Jenny has the rest for herself, her gossip magazines and her nail polish kit. I earn our money and Jenny manages our home. Like I said, our relationship is divided into two territories. It's the transportation of goods and services and everything Jenny has to deal with.

So let's say you manage to follow all this excellent advice and the two of you reach the expiration date of your plan. Remember when I said, "Have a plan?" You just read the sex parts, didn't you? Okay, well let's say you decided you'd live with her for a year and figure out if you were ready for the next level. So now it's been a year and there have been squabbles, but no major turf battles. Things are going smoothly. Thanks to the Belushi book, your cohabitation is working. Now what?

Oh shit! Now what!?

Yeah, you're not going to like this, my friend. It's time to—come on; you are going to ruin the spine if you keep throwing the book away.

It's time to pop the question—Dude! Seriously!

CHAPTER FIFTEEN

THE NEXT ILLOGICAL STEP

Sometimes you got to believe
Before you can see the proof
You can wait all your lifetime
For one moment of truth
Sometimes all it takes is a leap of faith

—"Leap of Faith," Glen Clark & Gary Nicholson

You're in a clearing in the woods.

You're in a clearing in the woods, wearing dress shoes, nice pants and a pair of boxing gloves. It's dark out and you have no shirt on.

You're in a clearing in the woods, wearing dress shoes, nice pants and a pair of boxing gloves. It's dark out and you have no shirt on. Your vision is blurry because you've had way too much to drink, but through the moonlight you can see six of your best friends glaring at you from the other side of the clearing. They, too, are wearing boxing gloves.

You're in a clearing in the woods. Still feel like getting married?

You know what? Let's back it up.

Let's back it up to the first time you got this idea, the first time you looked deep into your lover's eyes and thought, *"My God. I want to marry this woman."* Now, don't worry if you haven't reached this point yet. It doesn't mean there's something wrong with you. In fact, it actually means the opposite—there's something right with you. But don't get cocky and skip this chapter, because let me tell you something—you will think this someday. I don't care who you are, someday this thought will run screaming through your mind like a streaker at hockey game—quick, stupid and ugly, but leaving quite an impression. Hell, George Clooney even thought it once. Hugh Hefner has thought it at least twice. I've thought it three times. And if you think you're more of a man than George Clooney, Hugh Hefner and me, then you can put this book down right now and go back to polishing your Super Bowl ring, Coach Ditka. But if you're not Mike Ditka, you're lying and you need to keep reading.

Because once you have the thought, it doesn't matter how many times you send out imaginary cops to tackle, beat and handcuff that streaker. He still keeps running through your mind. "Should I get engaged? Am I ready?" Well, I'll answer those questions with a series of questions. Think of them as your first test on the road to marriage. It may not be as easy as you think . . .

Are you over thirty-five? Okay, that one is easy. No man should get married before the age of thirty-five—even if he has mastered the first two sections of this book. You need time to become a man, and really great women are not attracted to boys. Waiting until your mid-thirties is not about trying to sleep with as many women as possible before you die, it's about taking the time to become a mature, well-grounded adult. You will always wish you had slept with more women. If you sleep with twenty women over the course of your lifetime, on your deathbed, you will say, "Damn. I should have slept with more." If you sleep with two hundred women over the course of your lifetime, you will say, "Damn. I should have slept with more." If you sleep with two thousand women over the course of your lifetime . . . well, then you'll just say, "Damn." So will your family. Your large, sprawling family.

If you're within throwing distance of two thousand women, cross that line first, then go back to thinking about marriage. If you're not—and if you haven't hit the mid-seven hundreds by the time you turn thirty, you're not—just make sure you're over thirty-five. If you're under thirty-five, you're not ready.

Are you out of breath? A friend of mine works in banking and one of his rules is, "Never make any decision when you're out of breath." It means don't get sucked into the emotion of a moment.

So you've thought, "I should marry her." Is it *real*? What I mean by that is this: Is it a true reflection of an honest desire that bursts forth like a wellspring of pure, romantic love? And what I mean by *that* is this: Did you think it during sex? 'Cause if you did, it doesn't count.

It doesn't count if you thought it right *after* sex, either. Or if you were drunk. Or in major trouble with your girl-friend. And it especially doesn't count if you're all three. Being drunk, postcoital and in trouble is not the best time to make a decision about anything. And I say that as the not-proud half-owner of a flower shop outside of Kissimmee, FL, so you should trust me on this point.

Oh, and it also doesn't count if you're in love. Yeah, yeah, I know. You love the girl. Yes, you should love your wife-to-be. I'm just saying don't pull out the ring if you're *in* love. There's a difference. That *in love* feeling is worse than being drunk in some ways. Guys *in love* run off to Vegas. Then two weeks later they're running back because, thank-fully, it's just as easy to get *divorced* in Nevada.

Is she pressuring you? Of course she is. But . . .

Is she *unfairly* pressuring you? There's a difference. The "ticking clock" is probably the best example of unfair pres-sure there is. Women will always tell you that their clock is ticking. Doesn't matter if they are twenty-two or forty-two. There's always some clock ticking—they have to be in a re-lationship, they have to get married, they have to have a kid, to say nothing of family, society, girlfriends and career. Sometimes their clock is ticking so loudly that they don't even hear what you say. Oh, you thought they were ignor-ing you? Wrong. ". . . tick, Tick, TICK, **TICK**, *TICK!*" is all they hear. They use their clock as leverage to pry you out of the twelve-cylinder sportscar of perpetual bachelorhood and into the affordable minivan of commitment. But remember: Her clock is not your clock! And if your version of where you want to be in five years is different from hers, pretending that they are the same does no good. If her clock is ticking too fast for you, get out! Leave her! Do *not* let her biology pressure you into getting married. Just go. Trust me, she'll survive. That's another important point:

Don't stay with her because she can't survive without you. I understand that this is difficult advice to follow, but the reality is, they will be fine. Women will kick and cry and scream to anyone within earshot (you, their friends, your friends, their mom . . . *your* mom if they can find her) for about a month. But then—and this is the difficult part for men to understand—they stop.

That's it. It's over. They're done with crying and they're done with you. They put the ice cream back in the freezer, put on some makeup and start selling tickets to the next show. The light goes back on and they start looking for another guy—if they haven't already.

Men, however, tend to do the opposite. For the first month they feel great. Better than great—commitment-free! They can come home from work, throw their socks anywhere but the laundry basket, sit down and watch four Jim Belushi movies in a row. They can go out drinking and *hit on whoever they want.* They can fall asleep fully clothed, on the couch, with a bowl of chili on their chests. They can get thrown out of a stadium and not get the angry, silent treatment (except from the cops in the front seat on the way to the station). For men, the first month out of a relationship is happier than any of the months in that relationship.

But then something starts to happen. The socks begin to pile up. Sleeping on the couch every night hurts your back after a while. And the judge sounds like he means it when he says, "Sentencing guidelines, my ass. One more 'Drunk and Disorderly' and you're going to San Quentin." And yes, eventually they run out of Jim Belushi movies for you to rent. Men start to feel lost.

They become lonely, hurt and helpless. They being to think, "If she wants me so bad, I should marry her." This is a very critical time. Unlike women, who cry for a month and find someone better, this is when men are most likely to come back with a ring. *Do not go near a jeweler.* And for God's sake stay out of shopping malls. Jewelry stores are smart. They're always next to a food court (a guy's first stop in a mall). If you can hold out one more month—just thirty short days—you will be free. You were drunk on love and you need to sober up. You were a junkie with a girlfriend habit, and you need to detox. It's not easy, in fact this next month will be the most difficult, but you have to do it. You simply cannot go back to her with a ring in your pocket. You can't. So don't.

Sadly, some guys just don't have the willpower. I'm a perfect example of this. My biggest fear with women was that they couldn't survive the hurt if I broke up with them. The ego I had on me! But you know what? All the girls I broke up with (or who broke up with me) survived just fine and are living great lives without me. Some of them are living great lives in houses I bought, but I digress.

Okay, last question . . .

Is the ring a Band-Aid? This is really what I'm getting at. Is the ring the next, honest step in your life as a man and as a possible husband, or is it a desperate Hail Mary pass late in the fourth quarter of a bad relationship? Rings make shitty Band-Aids. Eventually, the wound will reopen and you'll be right back where you started, only you'll be older, poorer and have less hair. Remember, rings do not solve problems. (Well, sometimes they do . . . actually, they can go a long way toward solving a *lot* of problems. But not engagement rings; they create a hell of a lot more problems than they solve.)

So. Are you ready? Well, if you take an honest look at yourself and your relationship by answering these questions, you'll know the answer. And you'll have passed the first test. Wait, forget it, I take that back. "Passed the first test" sounds too . . . encouraging, and I don't want to be in the business of encouraging men to go against their most basic instinct. But like I said before, eventually you'll think about getting married, whether I want you to or not. So let me put it another way: You haven't passed a test. You have tested "positive" for Engagement.

From here on out, things get a little dicey. Your actions will have consequences—permanent ones—so you need to be very careful. You mess up the proposal, you'll be getting grief about it for the rest of your life. Sure, once you get married, you'll be getting grief about everything for the rest of your life. But you don't want to give her too much ammo too soon. You don't want to turn your marriage into a defensive rear-guard action before it even starts. You'll want to wait until at least year three for that.

The first decision you have to make is whether to go public with your decision or keep it in-house. By public, I don't mean renting a small plane to fly over Soldier Field with a "JNY—WL U MRY ME?—JM" banner trailing behind. That would be stupid. And you'll look like a cheap ass for not springing for all the letters. I guess "semi-public" is a better way to put it. Or "Should I run it past my buddies first?," which is really the best way of putting it. Should you run this idea past your buddies first, or should you just take your "positive" Engagement test to the jewelry shop and buy the first ring you see?

Obviously, you should ask your buddies first. This is another one of those questions that is easy to answer but difficult to act on. How do you tell your buddies that you want to take your independence, your manhood, your right to openly store pornography next to the toilet and trade it in for an untested, unproven and unappealing lifestyle? This will be one of the most difficult parts of the entire engagement process. That's why I'm calling it the second test: Telling Your Buddies.

This won't be easy. It would be easier, in fact, to sit your friends down, look them in the eye and say, "Guys, I'm gay." After all, if they really are your friends, at the end of the day they won't care. Sure, they'll tease you—mercilessly, at first. Don't be surprised if your car is magically painted pink overnight. But you'll still be part of the group.

That's why saying "Guys, I'm getting engaged" is more difficult. In a way you're taking yourself out of the group, whether you like it or not. So on the difficulty scale, "Guys, I'm getting engaged" lies somewhere between, "Guys, I'm gay" and "Guys, I'm gay and I've been loving myself to the thought of your naked bodies for going on three years now."

Actually, now that I think about it, you might want to lead with that last one, then say, "Just kidding. I'm getting engaged. To a woman." They'll probably put you on their shoulders for a victory lap around the bar.

If you think you can get through the "I've been loving myself to you" sentence, be my guest. But I can't seriously recommend it, because they'll probably punch your lights out before you're done talking. No, the best thing to do in this case is meet them head-on. Gather everybody at the corner bar, buy them all a drink, sit down and lay it on the line. Then lean back and watch the shouting begin.

See, just like you, no man really wants to get married. Men always want their freedom; that's why it's hard for them to commit. Men hate commitment. At a restaurant a guy won't choose between the cheeseburger and barbecue beef until the last possible moment before the waitress turns and walks away from the table. I've been driving the same car for three years now and in the back of my head there's still a chance I'll take it back to the dealer at any moment.

(Who am I kidding? A 12-cylinder Mercedes, that's something I can commit to.) And no matter what their marital status, they'll fight like hell to keep you away from the altar. If they're still single, they'll hate to lose a dependable drinkin' buddy. If they're married, they'll throw up their hands and say, "Turn back! Turn back! For God's sake, man, do not enter here!"

But if you're still 150% sure you want to get married, you'll have to fight them. (Note: If you're only 100% sure you want to get married, DO NOT PROPOSE. If you're only 131% sure you want to get married, DO NOT PROPOSE. In fact, if you are anything below 150%, put the ring down and back away from the jewelry case. Now.) But you will have to fight them. And *how* you fight them will be a better sign that you've passed the second test than simply convincing them. Any man can take a position and irrationally stick to it in the face of all logical arguments. Hell, look at Fidel Castro. The Soviet Union fell *fifteen years ago*. A Chinese company just bought IBM. South Koreans spend their weekends at Tokyo Disney while North Koreans spend their weekends eating rocks. But Papa Fidel is still waving swords and sticking to his story about Communism being the wave of the future. Good luck with that one, pal.

Like I said, it's not *whether* you convince your buddies that getting married is a good idea, it's *how*. You know how guys are when they buy something that they really wanted? They're excited. They can't *wait* to tell their buddies about "what a good deal" they got. "Hey man, I got the 24 CD changer, the heated seats, alloy wheels and I got the salesman to throw in a dozen car washes for free. And get this: I don't even have to make my first payment for six months! Best of all, it comes with a two-year membership in the beer-of-the-month club." They're proud. They're stoked. They're convinced they got the Deal of the Century and they can't wait to rub everyone's face in it.

It should be the same with your woman. As A. Justin Sterling says, it's important that you see her as a "good deal." But more importantly, you need to see her as giving you *something you can't get anywhere else.* "Hey, man, I'm getting in on the ground floor of this one. She's got a great ass. She's really smart. She's loves steak, but her mom is skinny so the chances of her beefing up are minimal. And get this: I don't have to marry her for six months! But the best thing about her is that she's into threesomes!"

The big thing to remember about going to your guys is that one of the biggest problems men have is that they believe their own bullshit. If you fall into that category (and we all do at some time or another), it helps to have five buddies sitting around a table. It's the same as being in a bar. If five guys tell you that you're drunk, you need to give up your car keys. If five guys tell you that she doesn't love you, or that she is cheating on you, she isn't right for you and you need to listen to them.

However, if you truly have a healthy relationship, you need to sit down with your guys and tell them, "Look, I dig this chick and I want to marry her." If you can sell them, you are home free. And, for your own peace of mind, you should probably ask if any of them have slept with her.

If you can convince them that you're totally psyched about this woman and that you're getting a great deal, so great you just can't turn it down, you're halfway through the second test of Engagement. And if you actually believe what you're saying, well, then you've passed. (Unlike the first test of Engagement, it is not only possible to pass the second test, it is required.)

Congratulations! (I say "Congratulations" because I assume that even after the second test you're still at least 150% certain you want to get engaged. If that's not the case—STOP. Now.) Now it's time for The Proposal. For women, getting engaged is the beginning of "The Dream," "The Romantic Fantasy." (For men, it's the end of "The I'm As Cool As Frank and Deano Were Back In The Day Fantasy.") It is the man's job to create The Dream for the woman, and this starts with The Proposal. There are a lot of rules to follow when crafting your Proposal. For instance, it's a good idea to talk to her father before The Proposal. Especially if he is going to pay for the wedding.

Notice I didn't say "ask for permission." No amount of flowers and white linen can dress up the fact that you're talking about fucking his daughter. So you don't want to open the door to him saying no. Here's how you phrase it: "I'm going to ask your daughter to marry me. I'd like to know I have your blessing." I mean, you're going to propose anyway, whether this guy wants you to or not. But this way you're honoring him as a man, while showing him that you're capable of standing your ground.

But the most important rule of The Proposal is this: Give Her a Good Story. 'Cause everyone's going to ask.

Her girlfriends will ask. Her mother will ask. People she loves will ask so they can bask in the romantic glow. People she hates will ask so they can tell themselves that their story was or will be better. Every couple you ever go out with for the rest of your lives will ask. In fact, her whole family will ask, although her father and brothers probably won't care—unless you fuck it up, big-time. (But you won't do that, because I'm going to tell you how to avoid fucking it up, big-time, small-time or even medium-time.) I'm telling you, you'll hear it over and over again, "Soooooooooo . . . how did he propose?!" So you'd better have a good story.

The easiest way to make sure you've given her a good story is by making it all about her. You are merely the writer, director, producer and bit player of the proposal. She is the star. That's why I said flying a "JNY—WL U MRY ME?—JM" banner over Soldier Field is a bad idea, unless she works for the Bears. Or she's a pilot. Or the person who arranges the letters on the banners that trail behind airplanes. (Although if that's the case, it would be pretty damn hard to sneak that one by her. Waving your hand and saying, "No, no, it's probably a different Jenny . . . and a different Jim, too" probably won't cut it.) You have to make it about her. I'll give you an example from my own life to show you what I'm talking about.

With Jenny, I planned a romantic dinner on a private beach. I asked for directions to the beach, something real men never do. And the Gods of Men slapped me around pretty good for that one, 'cause we ended up wandering over half of Maui before finding the place. Once we got there, the private waiter who was taking care of us wouldn't shut up. He talked about the beach, his relatives, how his wife had been driving him nuts lately and how bad married life was in general. (Yeah, thanks for that, pal. Hell of a lead-in.) Worst of all, he kept responding to everything with lines from my movies. Jenny commented on how nice I looked, and he said, "The best thing that could happen to him is an industrial accident!" (*About Last Night.*) I'd ask for more butter. He'd reply, "No More! No More!" (*The Principal.*) Is dinner ready? "At this point, we don't know." (*About Last Night.*) Once he even said, "Cats and dogs living together!" (*Ghostbusters.*) He must have been hedging his bets in case I turned out to be Bill Murray. (Why the hell does everyone think I'm Bill Murray?)

As you can probably tell, this night violated the number one rule of engagements in every way possible. It couldn't have been more about me and less about Jenny if we'd been surrounded by screaming members of the Jim Belushi Fan Club. And, yes, before you even ask, there *are* enough members of the Jim Belushi Fan Club to surround a small dinner table. [Simone: Uh, you might want to verify that. By the way, how's Dion? Did he ever make bail? Graft, huh? . . . too bad . . . who would have thought a nice guy like him . . . Oh, well—JB]

Anyway, this waiter hovered and pampered us so closely that I didn't have a chance to pop the question! What I should've done is pop him. But he was a man doing his job, and you never get in the way of a man doing his job. Even when their "job" apparently involves pinching my cheeks and quoting *Curly Sue*—"Aren't you cute?" Screw it; I should have punched the guy. Lucky for him I'm incredibly cheap, so I probably won't fly back to Maui, track him down and show him some Central American prison tricks I picked up while shooting *Salvador.* (Although I could get James Woods to do it for a grand.)

Dinner was a disaster. So I called an audible. We walked back to the hotel bar, where I suggested we sit, listen to the band and have a cognac. By this time, I wasn't just nervous, I was a wreck. I began to panic: Two failed marriages. Over forty. Losing my hair. I had gotten lost—literally—on the way to proposing to my third wife. Not to mention that idiot waiter complaining about his own marriage troubles. Maybe it was a sign. Maybe he was just trying to warn me and I was about to make a horrible mistake and Jesus Christ is it hot in here somebody open a fucking window . . . I politely excused myself. I walked calmly to the bathroom. I bent over and I suavely puked my guts out.

But did I give up? Hell, no. I reached back to my college days and pulled off the greatest "Boot 'N' Rally" of my life. I cleaned myself up and got back in the game.

When we got back to our room, I brushed my teeth and suggested we sit out on the balcony. The moonlight was shining down on the most beautiful beach in the world, with the balmy air blowing over us. I started talking about what a great woman she was, how she really understood me and empowered me as a man. She was agreeing, saying things like "You are finally seeing that," "Of course, I love you for who you are" and "Who's been telling you this? Gus?" Finally, I pulled out the ring and popped the question, which she did not see coming at all. She was shocked. She didn't even look at the ring. She jumped on me, hugged me, kissed me and held me for what seemed like hours.

I kept waiting for her to run to the phone to call her mom and her girlfriends. You know what? She didn't call anybody until the next day. It was about her being with me . . . about us . . . about our relationship. The marriage wasn't about the ring or the status of being engaged; it was about her being with me. How cool is that chick? I knew I had the right girl.

At this point, I'm going to turn it over to my lovely wife, Jenny, so she can give you her side of the story:

Hi, there. I'm Jenny, Jim's wife. I certainly didn't expect it when Jim proposed to me. Of course I was absolutely thrilled and accepted right away. But that balcony was really dark and I couldn't get a good look at the ring until we went back inside. Jim must have been really nervous, or sick or something (I remember him using the bathroom a lot. Maybe dinner didn't agree with him. Did he tell you about our waiter? He was really, really funny!) because he just kept going on and on and on about how great we were, and how I made him feel and how much he loved me. It was really sweet, but after a while I was like, "Enough! Get me inside so I can look at this ring!" I think we were only out there for ten minutes. (It was worth the wait, though. The ring was *gorgeous!*) Take care, and thanks for reading!

(Sigh) No, no. Thank you, honey.

As you can see, I pretty much blew The Proposal. But I sure as hell made up for it that night, if you know what I'm saying. In fact, I'd like to turn it *back* over to Jenny so she can tell you her side of the story of that night:

Jim, my mother is going to read this book. I'm not telling that story.

Fine. But, take my word for it. We broke furniture that night. That reminds me—make sure you leave some time for engagement sex. So don't propose on a plane, unless it's a private jet or has spacious bathrooms. (And remember, people are going to ask about this, and the phrase, "Then we fucked in the bathroom" is not the fairy-tale ending she wants to tell at the rehearsal dinner.)

My point in all this is to say that, while I may not have given Jenny the best story in the world, at least I tried. And with the exception of the waiter, I had a lot of help along the way. Dinner for two on a private Maui beach. A romantic balcony overlooking the Pacific Ocean. Alcohol. In a way, my Proposal to Jenny was like a big-budget summer blockbuster. Not the best story, but the sets were amazing and the action sequences were jaw-dropping. Oh, yes. The action was truly spectacular. (Jenny: Jim!)

Anyway, if you have enough scratch to afford a private yacht off the coast of Monaco, your proposal is going to be fine. But if you're on a budget, well, think of your proposal less like a summer action blockbuster and more like a modest-but-charming independent movie. Make it small, make it unique. Give her a good story. And make it about her.

Now that you are committed—or at least committed to being committed—let me give you one thought to ponder: You are marrying her mother. You've heard it before, and it's true. Look at her mother, because that is what she will become in shape, form and content. There might be a slight variation, but not much, because a mother teaches her daughter how to be a woman—the right way or the wrong way. If her mother treats her father like a bitch, then she is going to treat you like a bitch. If her mother is a gossip, then she will be a gossip. And if her mother has a fat ass, then she's going to have a fat ass too. So watch for the flags before you propose.

(**Contingency plan: What to do if she says, "No."** You take a breath. You put the ring carefully back into your pocket. And then you run like hell. Literally. Turn around and start running. And then get in your car and drive away—drive very far and drive very fast. And you never, ever look back. Now, this should never, ever actually happen. Any guy who asks a girl for her hand in marriage and receives a "no" should not have been asking, and probably didn't run it past his buddies first. Either that, or his friends are assholes.)

A buddy of mine once asked me to be his best man. I was honored, but after two divorces, I was more than a little sour on the institution of marriage (this was obviously before I met Jenny). But I was game, and did what every best man is supposed to do: I got the groom snot-slinging drunk and took him to a place where he could see shaved box.

As the night wore on, I loaded the party into a limo and told them we had places to go to. Naturally, they all assumed we were off to see more strippers. While there would be some more nudity, it was not what they had in mind. Instead, my buddy was about to take The Final Test.

Per my instructions, the driver took the car to a secluded highway running through some woods way outside the city. At the appointed time, he pulled over, and I ushered our group out of the car. I walked to the trunk and took out a heavy duffel bag and handed it to my buddy.

"You wanna get married? Get used to holding the purse," I said.

I then led the party into the woods. We walked for twenty minutes. Everyone was drunk and wearing dress shoes. My buddy was struggling to keep this heavy bag up and asking what the hell was in it every three steps.

Finally, we came to a clearing, and I told him he could set the bag down. I had a few of the guys set up torches around the clearing. Then I had my buddy go to the far side of the clearing and take off his shirt.

I took my buddy's hands and stuck a pair of boxing gloves on him. Meanwhile, the rest of the bachelor party was putting on their own fighting mittens. We all stood on one side of the clearing; he stood on the other. Drunk and confused.

Then I said, "All right. You want to get married? Fine. Get in the limo. It's behind us. But to get there, you're going to have to get through us. And we're going to kick your ass. Because if you're not tough enough to take on twenty of your best friends, you're not tough enough to get married."

And then we all took turns beating on our drunken friend. No bones were broken. There were no visible cuts, though there were a few bruises. And after a shower and shave, he looked just fine for his wedding, though he did walk a little slower down the aisle. Paul later described it as the greatest night of his life. Then he married a beautiful and loving woman who, unfortunately for me, he did not pick out of a catalog (lost fifty bucks to Stevie B. on that one).

This is the Final Test.

You're in a clearing in the woods. You're wearing dress shoes, nice pants and a pair of boxing gloves. It's dark out and you have no shirt on. Your vision is blurry because you've had way too much to drink, but through the moonlight you can see six of your best friends glaring at you from the other side of the clearing. They, too, are wearing boxing gloves.

Still want to get married? Make it back to the limo.

CONCLUSION

MY EDITOR SAYS I NEED ONE OF THESE

It all ended too soon
When I checked out of your room
Had to leave you behind
With that empty bottle of wine
It was a night to remember
And I ain't lyin'
When I told you that I loved you
It was the truth at the time

—"Truth at the Time," Glen Clark

What I've had to say to you in these pages could quite possibly be the most important information put in a book since God sat down to write the Bible oh so long ago. All right, the second most important. I have instilled in you the kind of wisdom that can turn legions of girly men into fully functioning studs as masculine as Stevie B. Okay, probably none of you are going to become that masculine, but there will be dramatic improvements. You can certainly become as masculine as yours truly.

Now, I realize that you were initially skeptical that an actor could really enhance your life and provide the basic building blocks of male self-confidence—despite the fact that actors have become governors and presidents. Things got a little bumpy when you kept scoring a gentleman's C on the quizzes. All the while, you were picking up valuable tools that will provide real-life experience. You must have found it convincing when I solidified my case with anthropological evidence and backed it up with interpretations of the Constitution and classic episodes of *The Flintstones*. Undoubtedly, the clincher came when I outdid the Playboy Channel's Handy Guide to Sex. But you realized this wasn't just academic mumbo-jumbo found in self-help books when you faced your first problem with a woman and solved it by field-testing the use of Curly, Gandhi and Clint.

Yes, it's been quite a journey, and we've accomplished a lot. It's taken me forty years to gather the concepts for this book. Hopefully, it wasn't too much of a challenge for you to read the book. We've realigned your backbone and set you straight as a man. You will end up like Rocky, not Custer. No longer do you feel like a Special Teams player. You feel like one of the Monsters of the Midway. At the very least, you are probably a Cubs fan. You know that a man defines himself with his terms, and that the underside of your tongue is softer.

You have returned to hanging around other men to

reinvigorate your competitive spirit. But it's not all butt-slapping and beer-guzzling. No longer are you afraid to talk to your buddies about matters of the heart. You now know that if you show your wounds to a woman, she will feel unsafe. You've also learned how to give advice, deal with your buddy's shortcomings without being a critic, and bring a cadaver back to life. It used to be said that if money doesn't ruin a friendship, nothing will. My fellow men, I am here to tell you that an even truer sign of manly friendship than the almighty dollar is a guy who will help another guy through girl troubles. It's a guy you can call any time without feeling like a pest and ask him to recite Belushi's Five Rules to Climb Up From Rock-Bottom in the middle of the night.

I gave you the tools to meet a woman—the how, where, when and why. And by why, I mean not just to get laid, but to be man enough for a woman. But more importantly, you know how to keep a woman intrigued. You've also come to appreciate that women are smarter than we are, and you are going to let them use their smarts to manage your relationship. This won't stop you from being a good guest. You can still fart at will—and you will feel more freedom to pass gas now, so just make sure there are no open flames around.

By now, becoming this man that you almost were has helped you land a smart woman, who loves you for who you are and leaves you alone. And thanks to the back-of-the-tongue technique, you've even become a one-man pleasure machine.

Remember, the real reason a man stays in a relationship

is because the woman gives him something no one else can. What I got from Jenny was simple—kindness. Jenny is the kindest woman I know, certainly the kindest woman I've ever been with. She brings a hell of a lot more kindness to our marriage than I deserve. Actually, after surviving the decade of my life where I hit rock-bottom, maybe I do deserve it. Which is why she was the opportunity I couldn't pass on. I had no choice; it was a great deal.

And now, by taking what you've learned in these pages, you're ready to be a husband and a father, right? Hell, no. You're not even close. That's going to be an entirely different book. And it's going to cost you twice as much.

PERMISSIONS

"Angel" by Jim Belushi and Glen Clark. Copyright © Pending. Used by Permission. International Copyright Pending. All Rights Reserved.

"Big Bad John" by Jimmy Dean. Copyright © 1961 Sony/ATV Songs LLC. All rights administered by Sony/ATV Music Publishing, 8 Music Square West, Nashville, TN 37203. All rights reserved. Used by permission.

"Bless My Soul" by Jim Belushi and Glen Clark. Copyright © Pending. Used by Permission. International Copyright Pending. All Rights Reserved.

"Cadillac Man" by Jim Belushi and Glen Clark. Copyright © Pending. Used by Permission. International Copyright Pending. All Rights Reserved.

"Can't Get Out of It" by Jim Belushi and Glen Clark. Copyright © Pending. Used by Permission. International Copyright Pending. All Rights Reserved.

"Get Out of My Life" Words and Music by Allen Toussaint. Copyright © 1960 (Renewed 1988) SCREEN GEMS-EMI MUSIC INC. All Rights Reserved. International Copyright Secured. Used by Permission.

"Have Love Will Travel" written by Richard Berry. Published by American Berry Music (BMI). Used by Permission. All Rights Reserved.

"Hot Weather Blues" by Robert Dade, William Ford, and W. Thurman. Copyright © 2005 Paul M. Martin. Used by Permission. All Rights Reserved.

"If You Don't Leave Me Alone, I'm Gonna Find Somebody That Will," by Delbert McClinton and Sony Fortner. Copyright © Nasty Cat Music/Delbert McClinton Music (ASCAP) (Administered by Carol Vincent and Associates). All Rights Reserved. International Copyright Secured. Used by Permission.

"I'm Ready" written by Willie Dixon. Copyright © 1954, 1982 (renewed) HOOCHIE COOCHIE MUSIC (BMI) / Administered by BUG. Used by Permission. All Rights Reserved.

"Lament," by Dylan Thomas, from *The Poems of Dylan Thomas*. Copyright © 1952 by Dylan Thomas. Reprinted by permission of New Directions Publishing Corporation and David Higham Associates. All rights reserved.

"Leap of Faith" by Glen Clark and Gary Nicholson. Copyright © 1993 Sony/ATV Tunes LLC/Four Sons Music/KRLT Music on behalf of Glen Clark